W9-BZI-655

DO-IT-YOURSELF GUIDES

Step-By-Step
Interior Repairs

Quality tools to build your world.

ACKNOWLEDGEMENTS

Created by Creative Publishing international
in conjunction with WSP Marketing International Ltd.,
47 Valleybrook Drive, Don Mills, Ontario M3B 2S6,
Canada.

**Creative Publishing international
Book Development Staff**

Vikki Anderson
Shawn Binkowski
Steve Boman
Janice Cauley
Marcia Chambers
Maren Christensen
Paul Currie
Doug Deutscher
Melissa Erickson
Jacque Fletcher
John Fletcher
Brad Kissell
Janet Lawrence
Bill Nelson
Chuck Nields
Jon Simpson
Greg Wallace
Gina Wornson

Printed on Canadian paper by World Color
Book Services, USA.

Copyright© 1998 Creative Publishing international.
Copyright© 1998 Canadian Tire Corporation, Limited
with respect to Mastercraft photographs and trade-
marks.

All rights reserved. No part of this publication may be
reproduced, stored in an electronic retrieval system,
or transmitted in any form or by any means, electronic, mechanical, photocopying, recording, or otherwise, without the prior written permission of the
copyright owners.

ISBN 0-86573-760-6

This book provides useful instructions but
we cannot anticipate all of your working
conditions or the characteristics of your
materials and tools. For safety, you should
use caution, care and good judgement
when following the procedures described in
this book. Consider your own skill level and
the instructions and safety precautions
associated with the various tools and
materials shown.

Creative Publishing international, WSP
Marketing International Ltd., Canadian Tire
Corporation, Ltd., or the Canadian Tire
Associate Dealers do not assume any
responsibility for damage to property
or injury to persons as a result of the use
of the information contained in this book.

Before commencing any project, consult
your local Building Department for information on building permits, codes and other
laws, as they may apply to your project.

INTRODUCTION

The longer you live in your home, the more money you need to spend on repairs – especially if you have to hire professionals to do the work. *Step-By-Step Interior Repairs* will help you do this work yourself and will save you both time and money. This book will guide you through the most common repairs needed to keep your living spaces in great shape. You'll see which Mastercraft tools you need and the proper techniques for using them, as well as information about the best materials to choose for your repair projects.

Step-By-Step Interior Repairs is divided into sections covering major areas of interior home repair. Each section contains the kind of information you need to know before beginning repair projects, including how to work safely and any work area preparations you may need to make. Then, individual projects are demonstrated with detailed step-by-step instructions and full-colour photographs. Throughout each section you will find tips about tools, materials and project techniques that will make your work as simple and efficient as possible.

Now you can keep your home in good repair – and save time and money, too. Welcome to the world of Mastercraft Do-It-Yourself Guides!

TABLE OF CONTENTS

TOOLS

To successfully make the repair projects seen in this book you need the proper tools, and they are shown here. Quality tools, like Mastercraft, will serve your needs well. Keep hand tools protected and organized by storing them in a toolbox. This also will allow you to easily carry them to the project site. Shelves or cabinets are good locations for power tools and other specialty tools and supplies.

Basic hand tools: *caulk gun (A), putty knife (B), pry bar/nail puller (C), work gloves (D), ear protection (E), carpenter's square (F), level (G), work light (H), chisels (I), sponge (J), eye protection (K), pencil (L), felt-tipped pen (M), mallet (N), hammer (O), awl (P), file (Q), nail set (R), dust mask (S), chalk line (T), hex key wrenches (U), utility knife (V), sandpaper (W), needlenose pliers (X), Robo-Grip® pliers (Y), groove joint pliers (Z), screwdrivers (AA), clamps – bar & C (BB), hacksaw (CC), tape measure (DD), scissors (EE), handsaw (FF), stud finder (GG), straightedge (HH).*

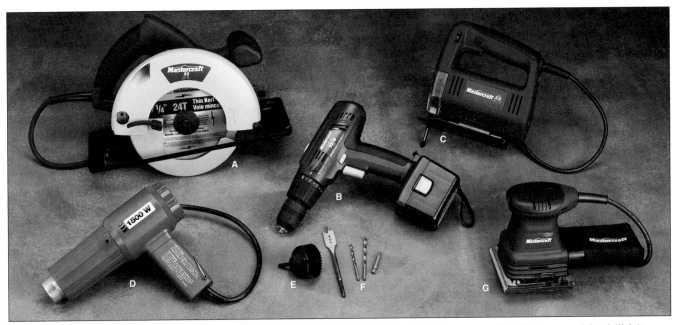

Power tools: *circular saw (A), drill, cordless or corded (B), jigsaw (C), heat gun (D), hole saw (E), drill bits, including screwdriver bits (F), palm sander (G).*

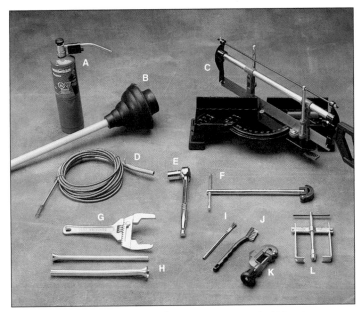

Specialty plumbing tools: *propane torch (A), plunger (B), mitre box (C), auger (D), ratchet wrench with socket (E), basin wrench (F), spud wrench (G), tubing benders (H), flux brush (I), wire brush (J), tubing cutter (K), handle puller (L).*

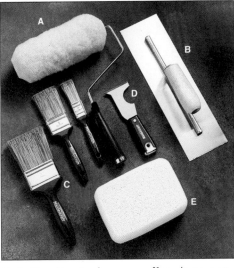

Painting/texturing supplies: *long-nap roller (A), trowel (B), brushes (C), combination paint scraper (D), sponge (E).*

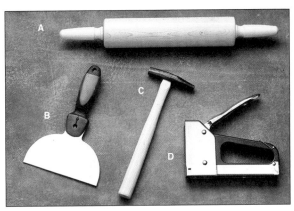

Other tools: *roller (A), taping knife (B), tack hammer (C), staple gun (D).*

WALL & CEILING REPAIRS

RECOMMENDED POWER TOOLS

DRILL

RECOMMENDED HAND TOOLS

- basic hand tools
- wallboard knife
- wallboard saw
- putty knife
- screwdriver bits
- carpenter's square

NEEDED MATERIALS

- wallboard tape
- wallboard compound
- Wall Bandages™
- latex bonding liquid
- rust-resistant primer
- surface filler
- shellac
- rubber gloves

- sandpaper
- plaster
- TSP (trisodium phosphate) cleaning solution
- bleach

Preparing wall surfaces before painting ensures a professional appearance and long-lasting finish. Preparation includes cleaning the surface to remove stains, dirt and grease, and repairing the surface of blemishes, including peeling paint, nail holes, popped nails, dents, holes and cracks.

Preparing Wall Surfaces for Cleaning & Repair

How to Remove Stains

1 Apply stain remover to a clean, dry cloth, and rub lightly to remove the stain.
2 Seal all stain areas with white pigmented shellac. Pigmented shellac prevents stains from bleeding through the new paint.

How to Remove Water & Rust Stains

1 Water and rust stains may indicate water damage. Check for leaking pipes and soft plaster, making repairs as needed.
2 Seal the stained area with a rust-resistant primer.

How to Remove Mildew

1 Kill the mildew spores by washing the area with bleach. Make sure to wear rubber gloves and eye protection.
2 After the bleach treatment, wash the mildew away with TSP solution, and rinse.

Fill Holes & Sand

Most repairs require you to apply surface filler and sand the areas you have prepared. Surface filler is best applied to the area using a putty or wallboard knife. You should choose a tool that is just wide enough to cover the affected area. Once the surface filler has dried, sand the area with 150-grit sandpaper until smooth and flush with the existing wall surface. 150-grit sandpaper is most effective because it has an open surface that does not clog.

How to Repair Peeling Paint

1 Scrape away loose paint with a putty knife or paint scraper.
2 Apply surface filler to the edges of the chipped paint. Sand the area smooth.

How to Repair Nail Holes

1 Apply lightweight surface filler to the nail hole with a small putty knife or your fingertip. Sand the area smooth.
2 Wipe dust away with a damp sponge, let dry, and paint with a rust-resistant primer.

How to Fix Popped Wallboard Nails

1 Drive a wallboard screw 2" away from the popped nail. Be sure the screw hits the stud or joist and pulls the wallboard tight against the framing.

2 Scrape away loose paint and wallboard compound surrounding the popped nail.

3 Drive the popped nail back into the framing so the head is sunk 1/32" below the surface of the wallboard. Do not set the nail with a punch.

4 Using a wallboard knife, apply three coats of pre-mixed wallboard compound to the nail and screw holes. Allow drying time after each coat, as the compound will shrink. Sand and spot-prime the patch area.

How to Repair Shallow Dents & Holes

1 Scrape or sand away any loose plaster, peeled paint or wallboard face paper to ensure a solid base for patching.

2 Fill hole with lightweight surface filler. Sand the patch until smooth.

How to Repair Small Holes

1 Inspect the damaged area for cracks around the edges of the hole. If there are no cracks, just fill the hole with surface filler, let dry, and sand it smooth.

2 If the edges are cracked, cover the hole with a Wall Bandage. The bandage has a mesh centre for strength and can be cut or shaped as needed. Wall Bandages are available in several sizes.

3 Cover the patch with surface filler or wallboard compound. Two coats may be needed. Let the patch set until it is nearly dry. Use a damp sponge or wallboard wet sander to smooth the repair area, eliminating dust caused by dry sanding.

How to Repair Large Holes

1 Outline the damaged area with a carpenter's square. Use a wallboard saw or jigsaw to cut away the damaged section.

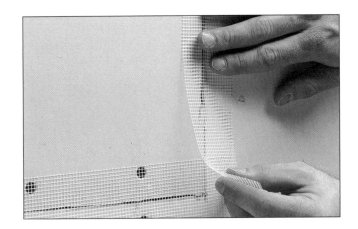

TIP:
Wash and sand surfaces before repainting. A solution of TSP and water can be used with a sponge to cut grease and remove dirt. Wear rubber gloves, and wash well, avoiding streaks. Rinse thoroughly with clean water. After drying, sand surfaces lightly.

2 Install wood or wallboard backer strips. For wood, use a wallboard screw gun or drill and 1¼" wallboard screws to secure the strip in place (photo above, top).
OPTION: Wallboard backers secured by hot glue can be used as an alternative to wood backer strips.

3 Screw or glue the wallboard patch in place over backer strips.

4 Apply wallboard tape to the edges of the patch (photo above, bottom). Apply wallboard compound, and sand the area (as in step 3, left).

Plaster Repair

Modern repair methods and materials have simplified the job of repairing holes in plaster. Coating the patch area with latex bonding liquid ensures a good bond and a tight, crack-free patch. Bonding liquid also eliminates the need to wet the plaster and lath to prevent premature drying and shrinkage.

How to Repair Plaster Cracks

1 Scrape away any texture or loose plaster around the crack.

2 Reinforce the crack with pre-gummed fibreglass wallboard tape.

3 Use a wallboard knife or trowel; apply surface filler or wallboard compound over tape so the tape is just concealed: if the compound is too thick, it will re-crack. Apply a second thin coat if necessary to conceal the tape edges (photo below).

4 Allow to dry, then sand lightly and prime the repair area. Retexture the surface.

How to Repair Plaster Holes

1 Sand or scrape any textured paint from the area around the hole.

2 Test the edges of the damaged area with a scraper to make sure the plaster is solid and tight. Scrape away any loose or soft plaster.

3 Apply latex bonding liquid liberally around the edges of the hole and over the base lath to ensure a crack-free bond between the old and new plaster.

4 Mix patching plaster as directed by the manufacturer. Use a wallboard knife or trowel to apply it to the hole. Fill shallow holes with a single coat of plaster.

5 For deeper holes, apply shallow first coat, then scratch a crosshatch pattern in wet plaster (photo above). Let the first coat dry, then apply second coat of plaster. Let the second coat dry, and sand lightly.

Texture Painting

Texture paints offer a decorating alternative to flat paints and wallcoverings. The variety of possible effects you can achieve is limited only by your imagination. Texture paints are available in either pre-mixed latex formulations or in dry powder form. Pre-mixed latex texture paints are fine for producing light stipple patterns, but powder textures are a better choice for creating heavier adobe or stucco finishes.

Using Texture Paints

Many tools can be used to create textures on wall surfaces.

Create a stomp design by pressing the flat end of a trowel into texture paint. Trowel over the texture pattern when the paint has partially dried, flatten the peaks, and achieve a brocade design (photo below). Clean trowel between strokes with a wet sponge.

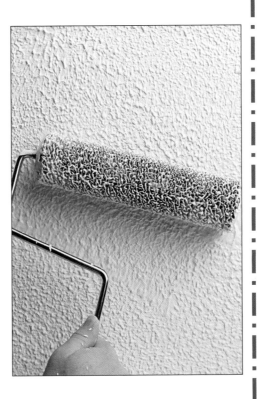

Create an adobe pattern by troweling texture material onto the surface and piling the material in ridges.

Make a stipple texture like those found on ceilings and stucco siding (photo above), using a long-nap roller. For different patterns, vary the pressure on the roller and the amount of texture paint on the surface.

Create crowsfoot designs by applying texture paint with a roller, brushing it out level, then randomly striking it with the flat side of a brush.

Create a variety of texturing effects by dragging, dabbing or swirling the sponge through the texture paint (photo right). Let the first coat dry, then sponge another colour on top for a two-tone stucco effect.

Create a swirl pattern with a whisk broom. Apply the texture paint with a roller, then use the broom to achieve the desired design.

TIPS:

Practise textures on heavy cardboard until you get the pattern you want. Remember that the depth of the texture depends on the stiffness of the texture paint, the amount applied to the surface and the type of tool used to create the texture.

❖❖❖❖❖❖❖❖❖❖❖❖

Use a Mastercraft 3/8" drill with a 5 amp motor and paint mixer bit to muscle through powdered texture mix.

CERAMIC TILE REPAIRS

Ceramic tile is durable and nearly maintenance free, but the grout between the tiles can deteriorate. Damaged grout offers the only point of water entry, and water penetration will destroy the tile base, and eventually the entire tile job.

Repair

How to Hang Tile Fixtures

1 Place a piece of masking tape over the spot where you want to drill.

2 Drill a hole for the anchor using a ceramic tile bit and ³⁄₈" variable-speed drill. The drill bit should be the same size as the anchor. To ensure the drill does not skip on the tile, use a low drill speed.

3 Tap a plastic or lead masonry anchor plug into the hole and use a screw to attach the fixture. Be careful not to chip the tile.

How to Remove & Replace Broken Tiles

1 Scrape away old grout between the tiles with a utility knife or awl.

2 Break the tile into small pieces with a chisel and hammer for easy removal (photo above). Scrape debris and old adhesive from hole with a utility knife or sharp scraper.

3 Test-fit the new piece of tile to be sure it sits flush with old tile. Spread adhesive on the back of the replacement tile. Place the tile in the hole and twist slightly to ensure contact with the wall. Use masking tape to hold the tile in place overnight.

TIPS:

To avoid stains and mineral build-up on tiles, use a bath towel to wipe down the tile walls after using the bath or shower. Use an exhaust fan to remove humid air and avoid mildew and moisture damage.

❖❖❖❖❖❖❖❖❖❖❖❖

Use a Mastercraft variable-speed drill at low speed with a ceramic tile bit to drill holes in ceramic tile to hang fixtures. The low speed will ensure a clean hole.

❖❖❖❖❖❖❖❖❖❖❖❖

Ceramic tile that dates before the 1960s was set in a masonry base, and repairs should be done by a professional. Remember to use protective eyewear whenever using a hammer and chisel.

RECOMMENDED HAND TOOLS

- basic hand tools
- caulk gun
- ceramic bit
- awl
- scraper
- chisel

RECOMMENDED POWER TOOLS

MASTERCRAFT

DRILL

NEEDED MATERIALS

- tub caulk
- grout
- tile adhesive
- replacement tile
- masking tape
- rubbing alcohol
- masonry anchor

4 Remove the masking tape. Apply pre-mixed tile grout with a sponge or grout float. Let grout set slightly. Wipe away the excess with a damp cloth.

5 Let the grout dry for about 1 hour. Polish the tile with a clean dry cloth to remove the powdery residue.

How to Regrout Ceramic Tile

1 Scrape out old grout with an awl or utility knife to leave a clean bed for the new grout. Remove and replace any broken tiles.

2 Clean and rinse the grout joints with a sponge (photo above). Choose a pre-mixed grout that is resistant to mildew and stains. Use a foam grout float or sponge to spread the grout over the entire surface. Work the grout well into the joints.

3 Let the grout set until firm, then wipe away excess with a damp cloth.

4 Let the grout dry completely. Wipe away powdery residue and polish the tiles with a dry soft cloth.

5 Apply caulk around the bathtub or shower stall. Do not use the tub or shower for 24 hours.

How to Recaulk around the Bathtub or Shower Stall

1 Scrape out the old grout or caulk with an awl or can opener. Wipe away soap scum from the joint with rubbing alcohol and a clean cloth.

2 Fill the tub with water so it will be heavy enough to pull the edges of the tub away from the tile.

3 Fill the joint with a flexible silicone or latex caulk (photo below). Wet your fingertip with cold water so the caulk won't stick to your finger, and smooth the caulk into a cove shape.

4 Let the caulk harden, according to manufacturer's directions, and trim any excess away with a utility knife.

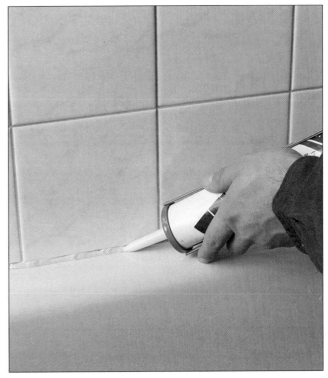

TIP:
Pre-formed peel-and-stick tub and tile caulks reduce the work of cleaning the joint and cleaning up the new caulk. Peel the backing off and press the new caulk into place.

DOOR & WINDOW REPAIRS

TIP:

Measure carefully when marking the door for cutting. Measure from the top of the carpeting, not from the floor.

RECOMMENDED POWER TOOLS

CIRCULAR SAW

RECOMMENDED HAND TOOLS

BASIC HAND TOOLS

- sawhorses
- straightedge
- chisel
- clamps

NEEDED MATERIALS

- carpenter's glue

Maintaining the integrity of your doors, windows and locks improves energy efficiency, security and the look of your home. Preventative maintenance, proper installation and repair will ensure the performance of your doors, windows and locks.

Sizing Interior Doors

Pre-hung interior doors are sized to allow a 3/4" gap between the bottom of the door and the floor. This gap lets the door swing without binding on the carpet or floor covering. If thicker carpeting or a larger threshold is installed, a small portion of the door may need to be cut off with a circular saw.

Wider cuts may be needed if a door is altered to fit a special installation, like a child's room or an undersized storage closet.

Hollow-core interior doors have a solid wood frame, with a hollow centre. If the entire bottom frame member is cut away when shortening the door, it can be reinserted to close the door cavity.

How to Cut Off an Interior Door

1 With the door in place, measure 3/8" up from the top of the floor covering and mark the door.

2 Remove the door from the hinges by removing the hinge pins.

3 Mark the cutting line with a straightedge. Cut through the door veneer on both faces of the door with a sharp utility knife to prevent it from chipping when the door is sawed.

4 Lay the door on sawhorses. Clamp a straightedge to the door as a cutting guide. Saw off the bottom of the door (photo above). The hollow core of the door may be exposed.

5 To replace a cut-off frame in the bottom of the door, chisel the veneer from both sides of the removed portion. Apply wood glue to the cut-off frame. Insert the frame into opening, and clamp into place. Wipe away excess glue and let dry overnight.

Freeing a Sticking Door

Doors stick when hinges sag or when the wood of the door or door frame swells or shifts.

Make sure the door hinge screws are tight. If a door continues to stick after you tighten the hinges, wait for dry weather to sand or plane the door. If the sticking problem occurs only during unusually wet weather, wait for a dry period, then seal the door edges. This should solve occasional sticking problems.

TIP:
Lubricate the hinge pins to eliminate squeaking in doors. Tighten hinge screws without removing the door by blocking up the bottom of the door with wood shims.

RECOMMENDED POWER TOOLS

PALM SANDER

RECOMMENDED HAND TOOLS

BASIC HAND TOOLS

- hand plane

NEEDED MATERIALS

- spray solvent/ lubricant
- wooden golf tees or dowels
- carpenter's glue
- sandpaper
- wood sealer

How to Fix a Sticking Door

1 Tighten any loose hinges.

2 If the sticking problem continues, use light pencil lines to mark the areas where the door sticks.

3 During dry weather, remove the door. Sand or plane the marked areas until the door fits (photo above).

4 Seal the ends and edges of the door with a clear wood sealer before rehanging the door.

How to Tighten Loose Hinges

1 Remove the door from hinges.

2 Tighten any loose screws. If the wood behind the hinge will not hold the screws, remove the hinges.

3 Coat wooden golf tees or dowels with glue, and drive them into the worn screw holes. Let the glue dry. Cut off excess wood.

4 Drill pilot holes in the new wood (photo above).

5 Rehang the hinge with the new wood as the base for the screws.

The extra safety provided by a good security lock is well worth the relatively inexpensive cost, and they are simple to install. A good security lock will have a latchbolt, also called a deadbolt (A) that extends at least 1". The latchbolt is moved in and out by a spindle (B) which is operated by a keyed cylinder (C) and a thumb latch (D). Some security locks use an additional keyed cylinder instead of a thumb latch.

RECOMMENDED POWER TOOLS

MASTERCRAFT

DRILL

RECOMMENDED HAND TOOLS

- basic hand tools
- hole saw attachment for drill
- spade bit
- chisel

NEEDED MATERIALS

- security lock (deadbolt)
- lockset
- spray solvent/ lubricant

Locks & Latches

Lockset Operation

Locksets operate by extending a latchbolt through a faceplate into a strike plate set into the doorframe. The latchbolt is moved back and forth by a spindle or connecting rod operated by a thumb latch, handle or keyed cylinder. If the doorknob or key binds when turned, the problem usually lies in the spindle and latchbolt mechanism. Cleaning and lubricating the moving parts will correct most problems.

Lockset Lubrication

Modern Passage Lockset

1 Remove the handles (held by the connecting screws or spring catch).

2 Loosen the retaining screws to remove the faceplate and latchbolt shaft.

3 Spray solvent/lubricant on all parts. Wipe away the excess lubricant; reassemble lockset.

Security Locks

1 Loosen the connecting screws to remove the inside and outside cylinders.

2 Loosen the retaining screws to remove the faceplate and latchbolt shaft.

3 Spray solvent/lubricant on all parts. Wipe away the excess lubricant; reassemble the lockset.

Lockset Installation

Installing a Security Lock

Security locks have long bolts that extend into the door jamb. They are also called deadbolts. The bolt of a security lock is moved in and out by a keyed mechanism.

Security locks help stop possible break-ins. Often home insurance rates can be lowered with the installation of security locks on exterior doors.

How to Install a Security Lock

1 Tape the cardboard template, supplied with the lockset, onto the door where the lock is to be installed.

2 Use a nail or awl to mark the centrepoints of the cylinder and latchbolt holes on the door.

3 Bore the cylinder hole with a hole saw and drill. To avoid splintering the wood, drill through one side until the hole saw pilot (mandrel) just comes out the other side. Remove the hole saw, then complete hole from opposite side of the door.

4 Use a spade bit and drill to bore latchbolt hole from the edge of the door into the cylinder hole (photo above right).

Make sure to keep the drill perpendicular to the door edge while drilling.

5 Cut a mortise (a rectangular hole with square sides and a flat bottom) for the strike plate with a chisel.

6 Bore latchbolt hole in the centre of the mortise with a spade bit.

7 Install the strike plate, using retaining screws provided with the lockset.

TIP:
The Mastercraft 3/8" drill with built-in level will ensure a level latchbolt hole.

Door Latch Repairs

Latching problems occur when the latchbolt binds within the faceplate or when the latchbolt does not slide smoothly into the strike-plate opening.

First make sure the lockset is clean and lubricated. If the latching problems continue, align the latchbolt and strike plate.

How to Align Latchbolt & Strike Plate

1 Fix any loose hinges, and test the door.

2 Fix minor alignment problems by filing the strike plate until the latchbolt fits.

3 Check the door for square fit. If the door is badly tilted, remove the door and shim the top or bottom hinge. Raise the position of the latchbolt by inserting a thin cardboard shim behind the bottom hinge (photo bottom right). To lower the latchbolt, shim behind the top hinge.

How to Straighten a Warped Door

1 Remove the door. Support both ends of the warped door on sawhorses.

2 Place heavy weights on bowed centre. Leave the door weighted for several days until the bow is straightened.

3 Check the door with a straightedge.

4 Apply clear sealer to the ends and edges of the door to prevent moisture from entering the wood in the future.

5 Rehang the door.

RECOMMENDED HAND TOOLS

MASTERCRAFT
BASIC HAND TOOLS

- metal file

NEEDED MATERIALS

- cardboard shims
- weights
- wood sealer

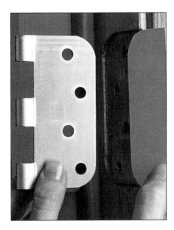

Repairing Windows & Doors

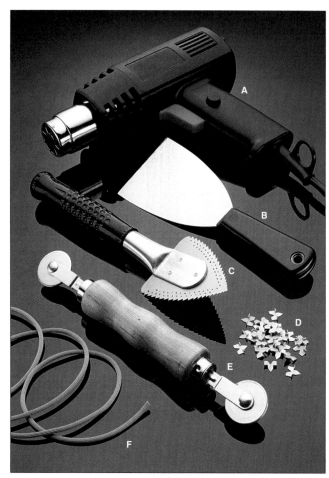

Tools for windows and doors: *heat gun (A), putty knife (B), paint zipper (C), glazing points (D), spine roller (E), spine (F).*

Eighty percent of all problems with window or door hardware are caused by a lack of lubrication.

Cleaning & Lubricating Tips

Clean the tracks on sliding windows and doors with a hand vacuum and a toothbrush. Dirt build-up is common on storm window tracks.

Clean weatherstrips by spraying with cleaner and wiping away dirt. Use paint solvent to remove paint that may bind windows. Apply a small amount of lubricant to prevent sticking.

Lubricate locksets and hinges once a year by taking them apart and spraying with solvent/lubricant. Lubricate new locksets before installing them.

How to Clean & Lubricate Sliding Doors

1 Clean the tracks with a toothbrush and damp cloth or hand vacuum.
2 Spray solvent/lubricant on all rollers.
3 Replace any bent or worn parts.
4 Check the gap along the bottom edge of the door to make sure it is even. To adjust the gap, rotate the mounting screw to raise or lower the door edge.

How to Lubricate & Adjust Bifold Doors

1 Open or remove doors and wipe tracks with a clean rag.
2 Spray the track and rollers or pins with greaseless lubricant.
3 Check closed doors for alignment within the door frame. If the gap between closed doors is not even, adjust the top pivot blocks with a screwdriver or wrench. Adjustable pivot blocks may be found at the bottom of some doors. Adjust pivot block until gap between door and frame is even.

How to Lubricate Garage Doors

1 Clean the rollers and the door tracks with a cloth, then spray with lubricant.
2 Tighten any loose screws, bolts or nuts.
3 Clean and lubricate the drive chain and track of an automatic opener.
4 Check manufacturer's instructions for additional maintenance directions.
CAUTION: Do not tamper with steel springs; they are under high tension and should be adjusted by a professional.

Weatherstripping

Weatherstripping seals cracks between jointed or moving materials, keeps dirt, insects and cold air outside of your house, and keeps conditioned air (heated or cooled) inside the home.

How to Install a Garage Door Weatherstrip

1 Remove cracked or brittle weatherstrip by prying out old nails.

2 Cut a new weatherstrip to fit the door, and nail strip to the bottom of the door with non-corroding galvanized nails.

How to Install a Door Sweep

1 Measure width of door, then cut a new sweep with a hacksaw so the sweep is 1/8" narrower than width of door.

2 Drill pilot holes for screws, then screw sweep to inside of door so the felt or vinyl blocks the gap under door (photo below). Adjust, using slotted screw holes in the sweep.

How to Install Spring-metal Door Stripping

1 Cut metal strips to fit the top and both sides of the door frame (jamb).

2 Open V of the strip faces outdoors. Nail the strips in place with a slight gap between the metal and the door stop. Spring metal compresses to seal air leaks when the door is closed.

3 Pry metal outward slightly with a screwdriver to ensure a tight seal. Do this before each heating season, as the strip gradually loosens its spring.

RECOMMENDED POWER TOOLS

MASTERCRAFT

DRILL

RECOMMENDED HAND TOOLS

MASTERCRAFT

BASIC HAND TOOLS

• tin snips
• hacksaw
• pry bar

NEEDED MATERIALS

• weatherstripping

How to Install Adhesive Vinyl V-stripping

1 Clean window sashes and channels with a dry cloth, and remove worn weatherstripping.

2 Cut vinyl v-strips for the window channels. Strips should measure 2" longer than the window sash. Crease each strip into a V shape.

3 Open lower window fully. Tuck top end of v-strips into cracks between window and channel, with open V facing outdoors. Peel off liner, beginning at the bottom, and press v-strip in place.

4 Cut a strip to fit bottom sash. Peel liner and press the v-strip onto bottom sash.

5 Cut v-strip to fit lock rail of the top window. Crease the strip, then peel the liner off. Press v-strip into place. Open V of the strip should face down.

How to Install Metal & Vinyl Stripping

1 Cut a strip of weatherstripping long enough so one piece will seal opening.

2 Bend the strip sharply to fit the corners. Press the strip against the window sash so that the vinyl compresses slightly.

3 Nail the weatherstripping around the opening. At the corners, nail close to the corner to ensure a tight seal.

Maintaining Storm Doors & Windows

Removable storm windows are excellent insulators when they are in good condition, and removable screens provide full ventilation. For these reasons many home owners still prefer them over combination storm and screen windows – even though they must be changed with the seasons.

Simple wood sash construction and a lack of moving parts make removable storm and screen windows easy to repair and maintain. Replacing screening or glass, tightening loose joints and applying fresh paint are the primary maintenance jobs.

Tips for Maintaining Storm Doors & Windows

❏ Tighten storm door latches by redriving loose screws in strike plate. If latch does not catch on strike plate, loosen screws on the strike plate, insert thin wood shims between the plate and jamb, and retighten screws.
❏ Add a wind chain if your storm door does not have one. Wind chains prevent doors from blowing open too far, causing damage to door hinges or closer. Set chains so the door will not open more than 90°.
❏ Adjust the door closer for the right amount of tension to close the door securely without slamming. Most closers have tension adjustment screws at the end of the cylinder farthest from the hinge side of the door.
❏ Replace turnbuttons and window clips that do not hold storm windows tightly in place. Fill old screw holes with wood putty or toothpicks and glue before driving screws.
❏ Lubricate sliding assemblies on metal-framed combination storm windows once a year, using penetrating lubricant.

RECOMMENDED POWER TOOLS

MASTERCRAFT

DRILL

RECOMMENDED HAND TOOLS

- basic hand tools
- clamps
- mallet
- putty knife
- staple gun
- tack hammer
- scissors
- chisel
- caulk gun
- pry bar

NEEDED MATERIALS

- epoxy glue
- dowels
- caulk
- replacement glass
- glazier's points
- glazing compound
- screening
- wire brads
- primer or sealer

Repairing Wood Storm Windows & Screens

How to Repair Loose Joints in Wood Sash Frames

1 Remove glass or screening, then carefully separate loose joint, using a flat pry bar.

2 Scrape mating surfaces clean. Inject epoxy glue into joint (plain wood glue should not be used for exterior work). Press mating surfaces back together and clamp with bar clamps. Frame should be square.

3 After the glue is dry, reinforce the repair by drilling two 3/16"-diameter holes through the joint (mortise-and-tenon joints are common). Cut two 3/16"-diameter dowels about 1" longer then the thickness of the frame, and round over one end of each dowel with sandpaper. Coat the dowels with epoxy glue, and drive them through the holes.

4 After glue dries, trim dowel ends back with a backsaw, then sand until they are flush with the sash. Touch up with paint.

How to Replace Glass in a Wood Storm Window

1 Clean out the recesses for glass and screening by carefully removing old glass, glazing compound and glazier's points (or screening and retaining strips).

2 Scrape residue from the recesses with a chisel, then paint with a coat of primer or sealer before installing new glass or screen.

3 Measuring from the outside shoulders of the glass recess, measure the full width and height of the opening, subtract 1/8" from each dimension, and have new glass cut to fit.

4 Apply a thin bead of caulk in the recess to create a bed for the new pane of glass. Press the new glass pane into the fresh caulk (photo right).

5 Use a putty knife or slot screwdriver blade to push glazier's points into the frame every 8" to 10" to hold the glass in place.

6 Roll glazing compound into 3/8"-diameter "snakes" and press the snakes into the joint between the glass and the frame. Smooth the compound with a putty knife held at a 45° angle to create a flat surface.

7 Strip off the excess glazing compound. Let the compound dry for several days before painting.

How to Replace Screening in a Wood Storm Window

1 Completely clean and prepare the recess.

2 Cut a new piece of screening at least 3" longer in height and in width than the opening.

3 Tack the top edge of the screening into the recess with a staple gun. Stretch the screen tightly toward the bottom. Tack the bottom into the recess. Tack one side into place. Then, stretch the screening tightly across the frame, and tack the other side (photo right).

4 Attach retaining strips over the edges of the screening. Do not use old nail holes: drill 1/32"-diameter pilot holes in the retaining strips, then drive in 1" wire brads.

5 Trim off excess screening with a sharp utility knife.

TIPS:

Use fibreglass screening for residential windows – it is easy to work with and will not rust or corrode.

❖❖❖❖❖❖❖❖❖❖❖❖

A Mastercraft staple gun will ensure the screen is stretched securely over the storm window frame.

FLOOR REPAIRS

Taking the time to examine your existing floor is essential before beginning any floor repair or replacement. A careful evaluation will help you make informed decisions on whether repair or replacement is best and how to prepare the existing floor for new floor covering.

Evaluating your floor is a three-part process. First, identify the type of existing floor and determine how it was installed: Is your sheet vinyl attached with full spread adhesive, or is it fastened with a perimeter-bond adhesive? Is your carpet glued down, or stretched? Next, assess the condition of the floor: Is it securely adhered, or is it loose in spots? Is it badly chipped or cracked? Finally, note the height of your existing floor in relation to the adjoining floor surfaces.

> **TIP:**
> Prevent damage and excess wear on your floors by placing a door mat at each entry. The mat prevents tracking grit onto floors, reducing wear and the need for cleaning.

Quite often, a new floor covering or new underlayment can be installed on top of the existing flooring. Your evaluation, in conjunction with the information in this section, will help you determine if this is possible.

WARNING: Resilient flooring manufactured before 1986 probably contains asbestos, which can cause several lung problems if inhaled. The recommended method for dealing with asbestos-laden resilient flooring is to cover it with an underlayment. If it must be removed, do not attempt to do the work yourself. Instead, consult a certified asbestos-abatement contractor.

Evaluating an Existing Floor

Your floor consists of these components: *floor covering (A), adhesive (B), underlayment (C), subfloor (D), and joist (E).*

The anatomy of your floor:
A floor is composed of several layers that work together to provide the required structural support and desired appearance. At the bottom of it all are the joists, the sturdy framing elements that provide the support for the weight of the floor. Joists are typically spaced 16" apart on centre. Nailed to the joists is the subfloor. Most subfloors installed in the 1970s or later are made of 3/4" tongue-and-groove plywood, but in older homes, the subfloor often consists of 1" wood planks nailed diagonally across the floor joists. On top of the subfloor, most builders place a layer of 1/2" thick plywood underlayment. For many types of floor coverings, adhesive or mortar is spread on the underlayment before the floor covering is installed.

Floor Repairs

The most common floor repairs include removing burns or stains from carpet or hardwood, replacing or repairing damaged vinyl, restoring damaged or stained hardwood and silencing floors and stairs that squeak.

If you have saved the leftovers from a floor-covering installation, you already have the materials needed to repair small areas of damaged vinyl or carpeting. If you do not have remnants, take patch material from an inconspicuous area – a carpeted closet or the tiled area behind a kitchen appliance.

Rental stores have specialty tools such as power stretchers, glue irons and edge trimmers for carpet repairs and installation. Describe the problem and ask the rental clerk to suggest the right tools for your project.

Silencing Squeaking Floors & Stairs

Floors and stairs squeak when wooden floorboards or structural beams rub against each other. The X-bridging (wood braces) between the joists can squeak when the floor above flexes under traffic. Floorboards may squeak when they have not been properly nailed to the subfloor. Water pipes or air ducts may also rub against the floor joists.

When possible, fix squeaks from underneath the floor or staircase. If the floor or staircase is covered by a finished ceiling, work on squeaks from the top side. With hardwood floors, drive finish nails into the seams between planks to silence squeaking. With floors covered by carpeting or linoleum, fix the squeaks when replacing the floor covering.

RECOMMENDED HAND TOOLS

MASTERCRAFT

BASIC HAND TOOLS

- caulk gun
- nail set

NEEDED MATERIALS

- 1" wood screws
- carpenter's glue
- hardwood wedges
- construction adhesive
- wood blocks
- flooring nails

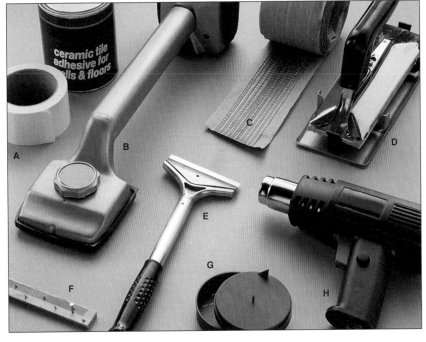

Tools and materials for floor repair: *double-face tape (A), knee kicker (B), heat-activated carpet tape (C), seam iron (D), razor scraper (E), tackless strip (F), "cookie cutter" (G), heat gun (H).*

TIP:
Use a Mastercraft cordless drill with a screwdriver bit to make overhead tasks easier, such as driving wood screws through the subfloor into hardwood flooring.

RECOMMENDED POWER TOOLS

• seam iron

RECOMMENDED HAND TOOLS

MASTERCRAFT

BASIC HAND TOOLS

• cookie-cutter carpet tool
• knee kicker

NEEDED MATERIALS

• double-face tape
• seam adhesive
• heat-activated tape

Three Ways to Silence Squeaking Floors

Check pipe hangers, heating ducts and X-bridging for rubbing. Loosen tight pipe hangers and separate wooden bridging to eliminate any rubbing.

Drive wood screws to draw hardwood flooring and subfloor together and stop them from squeaking. Make sure the screws are not too long.

Cut hardwood wedges and drive the wedges between the joists and subfloor to prevent flexing of the floor (photo left).

Three Ways to Silence Squeaking Stairs

Glue wood blocks with construction adhesive underneath stairs to reinforce the joints between the treads and risers. After gluing, secure the wood blocks with wood screws.

Cut hardwood wedges and coat them with carpenter's glue. Drive the wedges between the treads and risers to tighten the joints and stop squeaks.

Anchor treads to risers by driving flooring nails at opposite angles to prevent loosening (photo below).

Repairing Carpeting

Stains and burns are the most common carpeting problems. If you cannot remove a stain, you usually can patch the carpeting by cutting away the damaged area and inserting a new piece of carpet. With superficial burns, clip away burned fibres with fingernail scissors.

Another common problem is carpet seams or edges that have come loose. You can rent tools to fix all of the problems shown on these pages.

How to Repair Burned or Stained Carpet

1 Remove extensive damage or stain with "cookie-cutter" tool, available at carpeting stores. Press the cutter down over damaged area and twist to cut away carpet.

2 Cut a replacement patch from scrap carpeting using the cookie cutter.

3 Insert double-face carpet tape under the carpet so that the tape overlaps the patch seam. Press the patch into place (photo above). Make sure the direction of the nap or pattern matches the existing carpet.

4 Seal the seam with seam adhesive to prevent unravelling.

How to Restretch Loose Carpeting

1 Adjust the head of the knee kicker so that the prongs reach through to carpet backing.

2 Press the head of the kicker into the carpet about 2" away from the wall.

3 Press firmly with your knee to stretch the carpeting over and down onto the tackless strip.

4 Tuck the carpeting over the strip with a putty knife (photo right). If necessary, trim the excess carpeting. The carpet backing is held by the points on the strip.

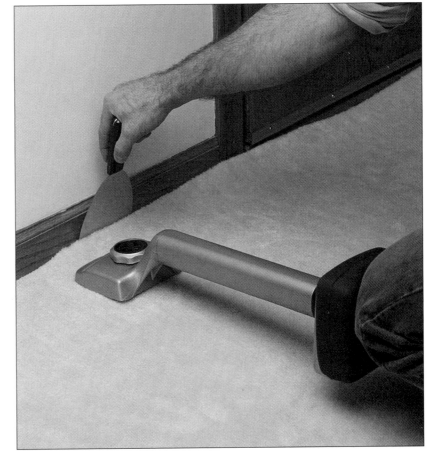

How to Reglue Loose Seams

1 Remove the old tape from under the carpet seam.

2 Cut a new piece of heat-activated carpet tape to fit the seam. Place the tape under the carpeting so that both carpet edges overlap the tape (photo right).

3 Seal the seam using a rented seam iron. Run the heated iron along the tape under the carpeting to activate the glue. As the iron moves along, press down on the seam to seal the edges of the carpet.

RECOMMENDED HAND TOOLS

BASIC HAND TOOLS

- carpenter's square
- putty knife
- razor scraper
- roller (a rolling pin will do)

NEEDED MATERIALS

- scrap floor covering
- masking tape
- odourless mineral spirits
- floor covering adhesive

RECOMMENDED POWER TOOLS

- heat gun

RECOMMENDED HAND TOOLS

- basic hand tools
- putty knife
- notched trowel
- roller (a rolling pin will do)

NEEDED MATERIALS

- odourless mineral spirits
- replacement floor tile
- floor covering adhesive

Repairing Vinyl Floor Covering

Deep scratches or tears in vinyl floor coverings can usually be repaired if you have patch material that matches the damaged vinyl. Patterned floor coverings like simulated brick or stone are easy to repair, because the edges of the patch are concealed by the pattern. If necessary, remove vinyl from a hidden area to use as patch material.

Replacing Vinyl Floor Tiles

Replace individual floor tiles when they become buckled, cracked or when they are badly stained. If you cannot find replacement tiles at a home centre, remove a tile from a hidden area such as inside a closet or behind a kitchen appliance. Older tiles made of asphalt may have asbestos fibres in the backing. Because asbestos poses a health risk, have a professional replace the floor covering.

How to Replace Vinyl Floor Covering

1 Select scrap vinyl that matches the existing floor. Place the scrap over the damaged area and adjust it until the pattern matches.

2 Tape the patch to the floor. Use a carpenter's square to outline the patch. Draw along the pattern lines to conceal the patch seams.

3 Use a utility knife to cut through both layers of vinyl. Lift out the damaged vinyl with a putty knife.

4 Apply mineral spirits to dissolve the old adhesive, then scrape clean with a putty knife or razor scraper.

5 Apply new adhesive to the patch, then fit the patch into the hole (photo left). Use a roller on the new vinyl to ensure a good bond. Wipe away any excess adhesive.

How to Replace Vinyl Tiles

1 Use a heat gun to heat the tile and soften the underlying adhesive. Be careful not to melt the tile.

2 Lift the tile out with a putty knife. Apply mineral spirits to dissolve the floor covering adhesive. Scrape away all of the adhesive with a putty knife or razor scraper.

3 Apply adhesive to underlayment. Position the tile in the hole. Use a roller on the tile to ensure a good bond. Wipe away the excess adhesive.

Repairing Hardwood Floors

Repair scratches and holes in hardwood floors with a latex wood patch (available in various wood tones), and remove stains with oxalic acid, available at home centres or paint stores. For routine cleaning and renewing, choose a hardwood floor kit containing wood cleaner, restorer and application cloth.

Give hardwood a coat of protective wax/cleaner twice yearly to guard against scratches and water damage. Always use solvent-type cleaners on hardwood: water-based cleaners can blacken the wood.

RECOMMENDED POWER TOOLS

MASTERCRAFT

PALM SANDER

RECOMMENDED HAND TOOLS

- basic hand tools
- putty knife

NEEDED MATERIALS

- latex wood patch
- wood restorer
- rubber gloves
- oxalic acid
- vinegar
- wood cleaner
- combination wax/cleaner
- 120-grit sandpaper

How to Patch Hardwood Floors

1 Apply a latex wood patch to fill in scratches, staple marks or nail holes in hardwood floors.

2 Sand the wood patch smooth with a palm sander. Sand in the direction of the wood grain (photo right).

3 Apply the wood restorer with a clean cloth and blend it into the existing finish.

How to Remove Stains from Hardwood Floors

1 Sand the stain area to remove the old finish.

2 Wearing rubber gloves, pour oxalic acid on the stain and let stand for one hour to bleach the stain out of the wood. Repeat if necessary.

3 Rinse the stain area with white vinegar. Let the wood dry completely.

4 Coat the bleached wood with wood restorer. Apply several coats of restorer until the floor matches the old finish.

How to Clean & Renew Hardwood Floors

1 Vacuum the hardwood floor to remove grit and dirt.

2 Pour wood cleaner from a kit on worn areas of the floor. When renewing an entire room, divide the floor into 3'x3' sections.

3 Rub over the area with a dry cloth or fine steel wool.

4 Let the floor dry, then buff the wood by hand or with a buffing machine. Apply a combination wax/cleaner or paste wax, then wax twice yearly for extra protection.

Safety should be the primary concern of anyone working with electricity. Although most household electrical repairs are simple and straightforward, always use caution and good judgement when working with electrical wiring or devices. Common sense can prevent accidents.

> The basic rule of safety is: Always turn off the power to the area or device you are working on.

Safety Tips

❏ Shut off the power to the proper circuit at the fuse box or main service panel before beginning work.

❏ Make a map of your household electrical circuits to help you turn the proper circuits on and off for electrical repairs.

❏ Close the service panel door and post a warning sign to prevent others from turning on the power while you are working on electrical projects.

❏ Never attempt an electrical project beyond your skill or confidence level.

❏ Never attempt to repair or replace your main service panel or service entrance head. These are jobs for a qualified electrician and require that the power company shut off the power to your house.

❏ Keep a flashlight near the main service panel. Check the flashlight batteries regularly.

❏ Always check for power at the fixture you are servicing before you begin any work.

❏ Use only UL-approved electrical parts or devices. These devices have been tested for safety by the Underwriters Laboratories.

❏ Protect children with receptacle caps or childproof covers.

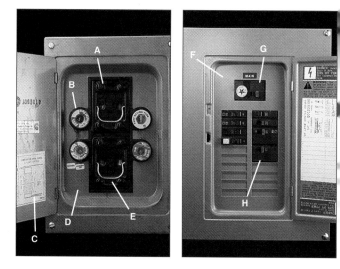

Fuse box (left): main fuse block (A), plug fuse (B), panel index (C), protective cover (D), appliance fuse block (E). **Circuit breaker panel** (right): protective cover (F), main circuit breaker (G), circuit breaker (H).

❏ Wear rubber-soled shoes while working on electrical projects. On damp floors, stand on a rubber mat or dry boards.

❏ Use fibreglass or wood ladders when making routine household repairs near the service head.

❏ Use GFCI receptacles (ground-fault circuit-interrupters) where specified by local electrical codes.

❏ Use extension cords only for temporary connections. Never place them underneath rugs or fasten them to walls, baseboards or other surfaces.

❏ Use the correct fuses or breakers in the main service panel (photos above). Never install a fuse or breaker that has a higher amperage rating than the circuit wires.

❏ Do not touch metal pipes, faucets or fixtures while working with electricity. The metal may provide a grounding path, allowing electrical current to flow through your body.

❏ Never alter the prongs of a plug to fit a receptacle. If possible, install a grounded receptacle.

Basic Electrical Know-how

Electricity flows through your home's wiring system much like water flows through a network of hoses. Each electrical circuit contains a "hot" wire, usually coloured black, which moves electricity outward from the main service panel. A second "neutral" wire, usually coloured white, carries the current back to the source.

Making electrical repairs usually means replacing plugs, outlets, switches or light fixtures. Electrical repairs are completely safe as long as you shut off the power to the wires and components you touch.

If an appliance is not working, check to see if the cord is plugged into an outlet. Appliance manufacturers report that in more than half of all service calls, the problem is an unplugged appliance.

TIP:
Double-insulated Mastercraft tools have non-conductive plastic bodies to prevent shocks caused by short circuits. Because of these features, double-insulated tools can be used safely with ungrounded receptacles.

Tools for Electrical Repairs

Home electrical repairs require only a few inexpensive tools (photo below). A good set of screwdrivers, a combination tool and needlenose pliers will usually suffice for basic electrical repairs.

Depending on the project, one may want to invest in testing tools. Testing tools ensure the continuity of the circuit and personal safety. Such tools include: neon circuit testers, continuity testers and multi-testers.

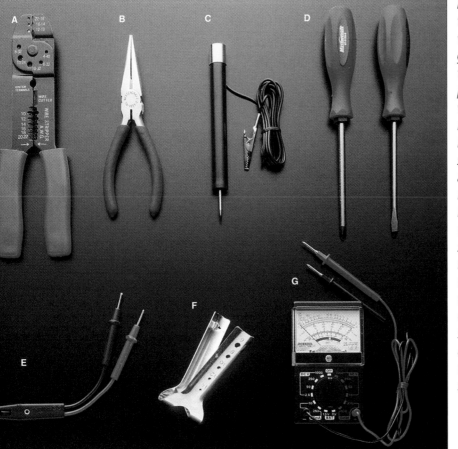

Basic tools: *combination tool (A) cuts cables and individual wires, measures wire gauges and strips the insulation from wires; needlenose pliers (B) bends and shapes wires for making screw terminal connections; continuity tester (C) is used to check switches, lighting fixtures and other devices for faults; insulated screwdrivers (D) have rubber-coated handles that reduce the risk of shock; neon circuit tester (E) is used to check circuit wires for power; cable ripper (F) fits over NM (non-metallic) cable to help remove vinyl sheathing; multi-tester (G) is a versatile, battery-operated tool frequently used to measure electrical voltages.*

Wires & Cables

Wires are made with copper, aluminum or aluminum covered with a thin layer of copper. Solid copper wires are the best conductor of electricity and are the most widely used. Aluminum and copper-covered aluminum wires require special installation techniques performed by professionals.

A group of two or more wires enclosed in a metal, rubber or plastic sheath is called a cable. The sheath protects the wires from damage. Metal conduit also protects wires but is not considered a cable.

Individual wires are covered with rubber or plastic vinyl insulation. Before 1965, wires and cables were insulated with rubber. Rubber insulation has a life expectancy of about 25 years. Old insulation that is cracked or damaged can be reinforced temporarily by wrapping the wire with plastic electrical tape. However, old wiring with cracked or damaged insulation should be inspected by a qualified electrician to make sure it is safe.

Wires must be large enough for the amperage rating on the circuit (chart, opposite page). A wire that is too small can become dangerously hot. Wire type designation is determined by the (CSA) Canadian Standards Association. To check the size of a wire, use the wire stripper opening of the combination tool as a guide.

Individual wires are colour coded to identify their function. In some circuit installations, the white wire serves as a hot wire that carries voltage. If so, this white wire may be labelled with black tape or paint to identify it as a hot wire.

Wire Colour Chart

Wire Colour		Function
	White	Neutral wire carrying current at zero voltage.
	Black	Hot wire carrying current at full voltage.
	Red	Hot wire carrying current at full voltage.
	White, Black Markings	Hot wire carrying current at full voltage.
	Green	Serves as a grounding pathway.
	Bare Copper	Serves as a grounding pathway.

Wire Size Chart

Wire sizes (shown actual size) are categorized by the Canadian Standards Association. The larger the wire size, the smaller the CSA number.

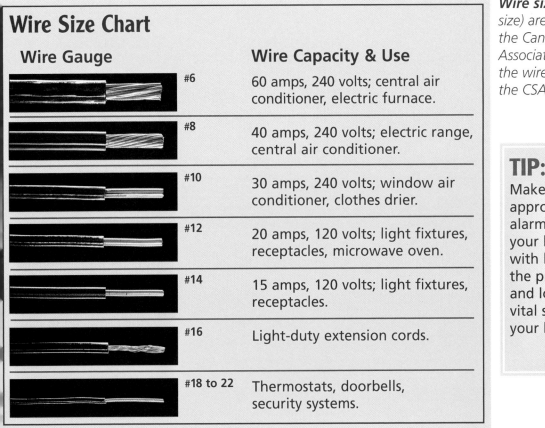

Wire Gauge		Wire Capacity & Use
	#6	60 amps, 240 volts; central air conditioner, electric furnace.
	#8	40 amps, 240 volts; electric range, central air conditioner.
	#10	30 amps, 240 volts; window air conditioner, clothes drier.
	#12	20 amps, 120 volts; light fixtures, receptacles, microwave oven.
	#14	15 amps, 120 volts; light fixtures, receptacles.
	#16	Light-duty extension cords.
	#18 to 22	Thermostats, doorbells, security systems.

TIP:
Make sure you have approved smoke alarms installed in your home. Check with local officials for the proper number and location of these vital safety devices in your home.

Reading NM (Non-metallic) Cable

NM (non-metallic) cable is sheathed in rubber or plastic and is labelled with the number of insulated wires it contains. The bare grounding wire is not counted. For example, a cable marked 14/2 G (or 14/2 WITH GROUND) contains two insulated 14-gauge wires, plus a bare copper grounding wire. A cable marked 14/3 WITH GROUND has three 14-gauge wires plus a grounding wire. NM cable also is stamped with the maximum voltage rating, as determined by the Underwriters Laboratories (UL). Inexpensive aluminum wire was used in place of copper in many wiring systems installed during the late 1960s and early 1970s, when copper prices were high. Aluminum wire is identified by its silver colour, and by the AL stamp on the cable sheathing. A variation, copper clad aluminum wire, has a thin coating of copper bonded to a solid aluminum core.

By the early 1970s, all-aluminum wire was found to pose a safety hazard if connected to a switch or receptacle with brass or copper screw terminals. Because aluminum expands and contracts at a different rate than copper or brass, the wire connections could become loose. In some instances, fires resulted.

Existing aluminum wiring in homes is considered safe if proper installation methods have been followed, and if the wires are connected to special switches and receptacles designed to be used with aluminum wire rated CO/ALR. If you have aluminum wire in your home, have a qualified inspector review the system. Copper-coated aluminum wire is not a hazard.

Basic Electrical Repairs

How to Strip NM (Non-metallic) Cables & Wires

Strip the insulation from each wire, using the stripper opening that matches the gauge of the wire; take care not to nick or scratch the ends of the wires.

How to Connect Wires to Screw Terminals

1 Strip about ¾" of the insulation from each wire, using a wire stripping tool. Choose the stripper opening that matches the gauge of the wire, then clamp the wire in the tool. Pull the wire firmly to remove the plastic insulation.

2 Form a C-shaped loop in the end of each wire, using needlenose pliers. The wire should have no scratches or nicks.

3 Hook each wire around the screw terminal so it forms a clockwise loop (photo right). Tighten the screws firmly. Insulation should just touch the head of the screw. Never place the ends of two wires underneath the same screw terminal. Instead, use a pigtail wire.

How to Connect Wires with Push-in Fittings

1 Mark the amount of insulation to be stripped from each wire, using the strip gauge on the back of the switch or receptacle.

2 Strip the wires using a combination tool. Never use push-in fittings with aluminum wiring.

3 Insert the bare copper wires firmly into the push-in fitting on the back of the switch or receptacle. When inserted, the wires should have no bare copper exposed.

4 To remove a wire from a push-in fitting, insert a small nail or screwdriver in the release opening next to the wire. The wire will pull out easily.

How to Connect Two or More Wires with a Wire Connector

1 Strip about ½" of insulation from each wire.

2 Hold the wires parallel, and twist them together in a clockwise direction, using needlenose pliers or a combination tool.

3 Screw the wire connector onto the twisted wires (photo above).

4 Tug gently on each wire to make sure it is secure. In a proper connection, no bare wire should be exposed past the bottom of the wire connector.

How to Pigtail Two or More Wires

A pigtail is a short piece of wire, with one end connecting to a screw terminal and the other end to circuit wires, using a wire connector. A pigtail also can be used to lengthen circuit wires that are too short.

A grounding pigtail has green insulation and is available with a pre-attached grounding screw. This grounding screw connects to a grounded metal electrical box. The end of the pigtail wire connects to the bare copper grounding wires with a wire connector.

Switches

Replacing Wall Switches

Most switch problems are caused by loose wire connections. If a fuse blows or a circuit breaker trips when a switch is turned on, a loose wire may be touching the metal box. Loose wires can also cause switches to overheat or buzz.

Switches sometimes fail because internal parts wear out. To check for wear, the switch must be removed entirely and tested for continuity. If the continuity test shows the switch is faulty, replace it.

Single-pole Wall Switches

A single-pole switch is the most common type of wall switch. It usually has ON-OFF markings on the switch lever. A single-pole switch has two screw terminals. Some types may also have a grounding screw. When installing, check to make sure the ON marking shows when the switch lever is up.

In a single-pole switch, a hot circuit wire is attached to each screw terminal. However, the colour and number of wires inside the switch box will vary depending upon the location of the switch on the electrical circuit.

If two cables enter the box, the switch is located in the middle of the circuit. Each cable has a white and black insulated wire, plus a bare copper grounding wire. The black wires are hot and are connected to the screw terminals on the switch. The white wires are neutral and are joined together with a wire connector. Grounding wires are pigtailed to the grounded box.

If one cable enters the box, the switch is at the end of the circuit. The cable has a white and a black insulated wire plus a bare copper grounding wire. In this installation, both of the insulated wires are hot. The white wire may be labelled with black tape or paint to identify it as a hot wire. The grounding wire is connected to the grounded metal box.

RECOMMENDED HAND TOOLS

MASTERCRAFT

BASIC HAND TOOLS

• neon circuit tester
• continuity tester
• combination tool

NEEDED MATERIALS

• fine sandpaper
• anti-oxidant paste (for aluminum wiring)

How to Fix or Replace a Single-pole Wall Switch

1 Turn off the power to the switch at the main service panel, then remove the switch coverplate.

2 Remove the mounting screws holding the switch to the electrical box.

3 Holding the mounting straps, carefully pull the switch from the box.

4 Test for power by touching one probe of the neon circuit tester to the grounded metal box or to the bare copper grounding wire, and touching the other probe to each screw terminal. The tester should not glow.

5 If the neon circuit tester glows, there is still power entering the box. Return to the service panel and turn off the correct circuit.

6 Disconnect the circuit wires and remove the switch.

7 Test switch for continuity and buy a replacement if the switch is faulty.

8 If the circuit wires are too short, lengthen them by adding pigtail wires.

9 If the wires are broken or nicked, clip off the damaged portion using the combination tool. Strip the wires so there is about ¾" of bare wire at the end of each wire.

10 Clean the bare copper wires with fine sandpaper if they appear darkened or dirty.

11 If the wires are aluminum, apply anti-oxidant paste before connecting the wires.

12 Connect the wires to the screw terminals on the switch. Tighten the screws firmly, but do not overtighten. Overtightening may strip the screw threads.

13 Remount the switch, carefully tucking the wires inside the box. Reattach the switch coverplate and turn the power on to the switch at the main service panel.

TIP:
Be careful not to touch any bare wires or screw terminals until the switch has been tested for power.

Three-way Wall Switches

Three-way wall switches have three screw terminals and do not have ON-OFF markings. Three-way switches are always installed in pairs and are used to control a set of lights from two locations. **One of the screw terminals on a three-way switch** is marked as the common screw terminal. Before disconnecting a three-way switch, always label the wire that is connected to the common terminal. It must be reconnected to the common terminal on a new switch. **The two remaining screw terminals** on a three-way switch are called the traveller terminals. Wires to the traveller terminals are interchangeable. **Because three-way switches are installed in pairs,** it sometimes is difficult to determine which of the switches is causing a problem. The switch that receives greater use is more likely to fail, but you may need to inspect both switches to find the source of the problem. **If two cables enter the box,** the switch is in the middle of the circuit (photo below). One cable has two wires plus a bare copper grounding wire; the other cable has three wires plus a ground. The black wire from the two-wire cable is connected to the common terminal. The red and black wires from the three-wire cable are connected to the traveller terminals. The white neutral wires are joined together with a wire connector, and the grounding wires are pigtailed to the grounded metal box. **If one cable enters the box,** the switch is at the end of the circuit. The cable has three wires, plus a bare copper grounding wire. The black wire must be connected to the common terminal. White and red wires are connected to the two traveller terminals. The bare copper grounding wire is connected to the grounded metal box.

How to Replace a Three-way Wall Switch

1 Turn off power to the switch at main service panel; remove switch coverplate and mounting screws.

2 Hold the mounting strap carefully; pull switch from box. Do not touch bare wires or screw terminals until power is tested.

3 Test the circuit for power by touching one probe of the neon circuit tester to the grounded metal box or to the bare copper grounding wire, and touching the other probe to each terminal.

4 The tester should not glow. If it does, there is still power entering the box. Return to service panel and turn off the correct circuit.

5 Locate the common terminal, and use masking tape to label the "common" wire attached to it. Disconnect wires and remove the switch.

6 Test the switch for continuity. If it tests faulty, buy a replacement.

7 Inspect wires for nicks and scratches. If necessary, clip and strip damaged wires.

8 Connect common wire to common terminal on the switch.

9 Connect remaining wires to the traveller terminals. These wires can be connected to either terminal.

10 Carefully tuck the wires into the box. Remount the switch and attach the coverplate. Turn on the power at the main service panel.

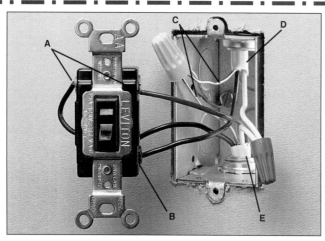

Typical three-way switch: *traveller screw terminals (A), common screw terminal (B), grounding wires (C), two-wire cable (D), three-wire cable (E).*

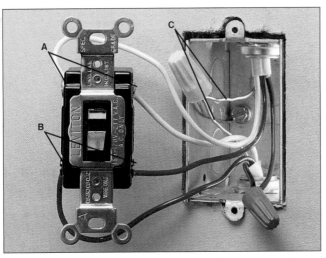

Typical four-way switch: brass screw terminals (A), copper screw terminals (B), grounding wires (C).

Four-way Wall Switches

Four-way switches have four screw terminals, and do not have ON-OFF markings. Four-way switches are always installed between a pair of three-way switches. This switch combination makes it possible to control a set of lights from three or more locations. Four-way switches are not common, but are sometimes found in homes with very large rooms or long hallways. In a typical installation (photo above), two pairs of colour-matched wires are connected to the four-way switch. To simplify installation, four-way switches have screw terminals that are paired by colour. One pair of screws is usually copper while the other is usually brass. Four wires are connected to a four-way switch. When installing the switch, match the wires to the screw terminals by colour. One pair of colour-matched wires is connected to the copper screw heads, while another pair is connected to the brass screw terminals. A third pair of wires is connected inside the box with a wire connector. The two bare copper grounding wires are pigtailed to the grounded metal box.

Double Switches

A double switch has two switch levers in a single housing. It is used to control two light fixtures or appliances from the same switch box. In most installations, both halves of the switch are powered by the same circuit. Installations where each half of the switch is powered by a separate circuit are more rare.

Single-circuit Wiring: Three black wires are attached to the switch (photo below). The black feed wire bringing power into the box is connected to the side of the switch that has a connecting tab. The wires carrying power out to the fixtures or appliances are connected to the side that does not have the connecting tab. The white neutral wires are connected together with a wire connector.

Separate-circuit Wiring: Four black wires are attached to the switch. Feed wires from the power source are attached to the side of the switch that has the connecting tab and the connecting tab is removed. Wires carrying power from switch to fixtures or appliances are connected to the side that does not have a connecting tab. White neutral wires are connected together with a wire connector. **To Remove the Connecting Tab:** Use a pair of needlenose pliers or a screwdriver.

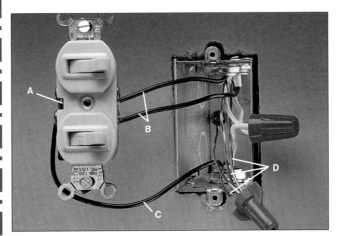

Double switch: connecting tab (A), wires to light fixtures (B), feed wire (C), grounding wires (D).

Receptacles

Common Receptacle Problems

Household receptacles, also called outlets, have no moving parts to wear out and usually last for many years without servicing. Most problems associated with receptacles are actually caused by faulty lamps and appliances, or their plugs and cords. However, the constant plugging in and removal of appliance cords can wear out the metal contacts inside a receptacle. Any receptacle that does not hold plugs firmly should be replaced. A loose wire connection is another possible problem. A loose wire can spark (called arcing), trip a circuit breaker or cause heat to build up in the receptacle box, creating a potential fire hazard.

The standard duplex receptacle has two halves for receiving plugs. Each half has a long (neutral) slot, a short (hot) slot and a U-shaped grounding hole. The slots fit the wide prong, narrow prong and grounding prong of a three-prong plug. This ensures that the connection between the receptacle and the plug will be polarized and grounded for safety.

Wires are attached to the receptacle at screw terminals or push-in fittings. A connection tab between the screw terminals allows for a variety of different wiring configurations. Receptacles also include mounting straps for attaching to electrical boxes.

Two-slot receptacles are often found in older homes. The black hot wires are connected to the brass screw terminals, and the white neutral wires are pigtailed to a silver screw terminal. Two-slot receptacles may be replaced with three-slot types, but only if a means of grounding exists at the receptacle box.

Stamps of approval from testing agencies are found on the front and back of the receptacle. Look for the symbol UL or UND.

LAB. INC. LIST to make sure the receptacle meets the strict standards of Underwriters Laboratories.

The receptacle is marked with ratings for maximum volts and amps. The common receptacle is marked 15A, 125V. Receptacles marked CU or COPPER are used with solid copper wire. Those marked CU-CLAD ONLY are used with copper-coated aluminum wire. Only receptacles marked with CO/ALR may be used with solid aluminum wiring. Receptacles marked AL/CU no longer may be used with aluminum wire according to Code.

TROUBLESHOOTING GUIDE

Problem 1: Circuit breaker trips repeatedly, or the fuse burns out immediately after being replaced.
Solution: Repair or replace worn or damaged lamp or appliance cord. Move lamps or appliances to other circuits to prevent overloads. Tighten any loose wire connections. Clean dirty or oxidized wire ends.

Problem 2: Lamp or appliance does not work.
Solution: Make sure the lamp or appliance is plugged in. Replace burned-out bulbs. Repair or replace worn or damaged lamp or appliance cord. Tighten any loose wire connections. Clean dirty oxidized wire ends. Repair or replace any faulty receptacle.

Problem 3: Receptacle does not hold plugs firmly.
Solution: Repair or replace worn or damaged plugs. Replace faulty receptacle.

Problem 4: Receptacle is warm to the touch, buzzes, or sparks when plugs are inserted or removed.
Solution: Move lamps or appliances to other circuits to prevent overloads. Tighten any loose wire connections. Clean dirty or oxidized wire ends. Replace faulty receptacle.

Receptacle Wiring

Wiring configurations may vary depending on the kind of receptacle used, the type of cable or the technique of the electrician installing the wiring. For dependable repairs or replacements, use masking tape and label each wire according to its location on the terminals of the existing receptacle.

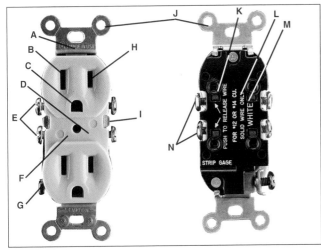

Front: *stamp of approval (A), long (neutral) slot (B), grounding hole (C), voltage rating (D), silver (neutral) screw terminals (E), amperage rating (F), green (grounding) screw terminal (G), short (hot) slot (H), connecting tab (I).* ***Back:*** *mounting strap (J), push-in fitting (K), wire ratings (L), wire type (M), brass (hot) screw terminals (N).*

Use a Neon Circuit Tester to Test for:

❏ Power to make sure that live voltage is not reaching the receptacle during a repair or replacement project.

❏ Grounding to plan receptacle replacements. The test for grounding will indicate how an existing receptacle is wired and whether a replacement receptacle should be a two-slot polarized receptacle, a grounded three-slot receptacle or a GFCI.

❏ Reversed hot and neutral wires to make sure the wires are installed correctly on the replacement receptacle.

❏ Hot wires if you need to confirm which wire is carrying live voltage.

Testing Receptacles for Power, Grounding & Polarity

When testing for power or grounding, always confirm any negative results (tester does not glow) by removing the coverplate and examining the receptacle to make sure all wires are intact and properly connected. Do not touch any wires without first turning off power at the main service panel.

MASTERCRAFT
BASIC HAND TOOLS

RECOMMENDED HAND TOOLS

• neon circuit tester

How to Test a Receptacle for Power

1 Turn off power at the main service panel.

2 Place one probe of tester in each slot of the receptacle. The tester should not glow. If it does glow, the correct circuit has not been turned off at the main service panel. Test both ends of a duplex receptacle.

3 Confirm power is off by removing coverplate and testing at the receptacle wires.

4 Remove receptacle coverplate. Loosen mounting screws and carefully pull receptacle from its box. Do not touch any wires.

5 Touch one probe of the neon tester to a brass screw terminal and one probe to a silver screw terminal. The tester should not glow. If it does, you must shut off the correct circuit at the service panel. If wires are connected to both sets of terminals, test both sets.

TIP:

When electricity flows through a neon circuit tester, the small bulb will glow. The tester only glows when it is part of a complete circuit. For example, if you touch one probe to a hot wire and do not touch anything with the other probe to complete the circuit, the tester will not glow, even though the hot wire is carrying power.

How to Test a Two-slot Receptacle for Grounding

1 With the power turned on, place one probe of the neon tester in each slot. The tester should glow. If it does not glow, then there is no power to the receptacle.

2 Place one probe of the neon tester in the short (hot) slot, and touch the other probe to the coverplate screw. The screw head must be free of paint, dirt and grease. If the tester glows, the receptacle box is grounded. If it does not glow, proceed to step 3.

3 Place one probe of the tester in the long (neutral) slot, and touch the other to the coverplate screw. If the tester glows, the receptacle box is grounded but hot and neutral wires are reversed. If the tester does not glow, the box is not grounded.

How to Test a Three-slot Receptacle for Grounding

1 With power on, place one probe of the tester in the short (hot) slot and the other in the U-shaped grounding hole. The tester should glow.

2 If it does not glow, place a probe in the long (neutral) slot and one in the grounding hole. If the tester glows, the hot and neutral wires are reversed.

3 If the tester does not glow in either position, the receptacle is not grounded.

How to Test for Hot Wires

1 With the power turned off, carefully separate all ends of wires so that they do not touch each other or anything else.

2 Restore power to the circuit at the main service panel.

3 Touch one probe of the neon tester to the bare grounding wire or grounded metal box and the other to the ends of each of the wires. Check all wires. If the tester glows, the wire is hot.

4 Label the hot wires for identification, and turn off power at the service panel before continuing work.

Repairing & Replacing Receptacles

RECOMMENDED HAND TOOLS

MASTERCRAFT

BASIC HAND TOOLS

- neon circuit tester
- felt-tipped pen

NEEDED MATERIALS

- vacuum cleaner
- fine sandpaper
- anti-oxidant paste
- masking tape

After shutting off the power to the receptacle circuit, remove the coverplate and inspect the receptacle for any obvious problems such as a loose or broken connection, or wire ends that are dirty or oxidized. Remember that a problem at one receptacle may affect other receptacles in the same circuit. If the cause of the faulty receptacle is not readily apparent, test other receptacles in the circuit for power.

When replacing a receptacle, check the amperage rating of the circuit at the main service panel. Buy a replacement with the correct amperage rating.

When installing a new receptacle, always test for grounding. Never install a three-slot receptacle where no grounding exists. Instead, install a two-slot polarized or GFCI receptacle.

How to Repair a Receptacle

1 Turn off the power at the main service panel. Test the receptacle for power with a neon circuit tester. Test both ends of a duplex receptacle. Remove the coverplate.

2 Remove the mounting screws that hold the receptacle to the box. Carefully pull the receptacle from the box. Take care not to touch any bare wires.

3 Confirm that the power to the receptacle is off, using a neon circuit tester. If wires are attached to both sets of screw terminals, test both sets. The tester should not glow. If it does, you must turn off the correct circuit at the service panel.

4 If the ends of the wires appear darkened or dirty, disconnect them one at a time, and clean them with fine sandpaper. If the wires are aluminum, apply an anti-oxidant paste before reconnecting.

5 Tighten all connections. Take care not to overtighten and strip the screws.

6 Check the box for dirt or dust and, if necessary, clean it with a vacuum cleaner and narrow nozzle attachment.

7 Reinstall receptacle, and turn on power at main service panel. Test receptacle for power with a neon circuit tester (photo left). If receptacle does not work, check other receptacles in circuit before replacing.

How to Replace a Receptacle

1 To replace a receptacle, repeat steps 1 to 3 of repairing a receptacle. With the power off, label each wire for its location on the receptacle screw terminals, using masking tape and a felt-tipped pen (photo below).

2 Disconnect all wires and remove the receptacle.

3 Replace the receptacle with one rated for the correct amperage and voltage. Replace the coverplate and turn on the power. Test receptacles with a neon circuit tester.

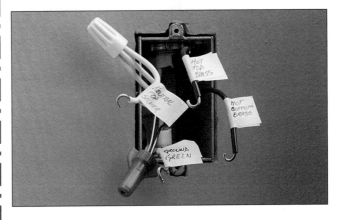

End-of-Run & Middle-of-Run Wiring

Receptacles are wired as either end-of-run or middle-of-run. These two basic configurations are easily identified by counting the number of cables entering the receptacle box. End-of-run wiring has only one cable, indicating that the circuit ends. Middle-of-run wiring has two cables, indicating that the circuit continues to other receptacles, switches or fixtures. **Single cable entering the box** indicates end-of-run wiring. The black hot wire is attached to a brass terminal and the white neutral wire is connected to a silver terminal. The grounding wire is either attached to the metal electrical box or to the grounding terminal of the receptacle. **Two cables entering the box** indicate middle-of-run wiring (photo right). Black hot wires are connected to brass terminals, and white neutral wires to silver terminals. The grounding wire is pigtailed to the grounding screws of the receptacle and the box.

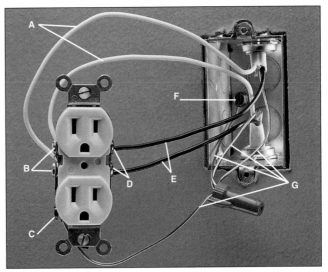

Middle-of-run wiring: *white neutral wires (A), silver screw terminals (B), grounding screw terminal (C), brass screw terminals (D), black hot wires (E), grounding screw (F), grounding wires (G).*

Split-circuit Wiring

Each half of the split-circuit receptacle is wired to a separate circuit. This allows two appliances of high wattage to be plugged into the same receptacle without blowing a fuse or tripping a breaker. This wiring configuration is similar to a receptacle that is controlled by a wall switch. Code requires a switch-controlled receptacle in any room that does not have a built-in light fixture operated by a wall switch. **A split-circuit receptacle is attached** to a black hot wire, a red hot wire, a white neutral wire and a bare grounding wire (photo below). Because the split-circuit receptacle is connected to two hot wires, one should use caution during repairs or replacements. Make sure the connecting tab between the hot terminals is removed. **Split-circuit wiring is similar to a switch-controlled receptacle.** The hot wires are attached to the brass terminals, and the connecting tab or fin between the brass terminals is removed. The white wire is attached to a silver terminal, and the connecting tab on the neutral side remains intact. The grounding wire is pigtailed to the grounding terminal of the receptacle, and the grounding screw is attached to the box.

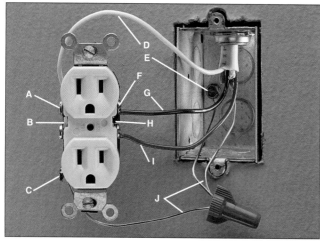

Split-circuit receptacle: *silver screw terminal (A), connecting tab intact (B), grounding screw terminal (C), white neutral wire (D), grounding screw (E), brass screw terminal (F), black hot wire (G), connecting tab removed (H), red hot wire (I), grounding wires (J).*

RECOMMENDED HAND TOOLS

MASTERCRAFT

BASIC HAND TOOLS

• combination tool
• needlenose pliers

NEEDED MATERIALS

• replacement plug

Replacing a Plug

Replace an electrical plug whenever you notice bent or loose prongs, a cracked or damaged casing or a missing insulating faceplate. A damaged plug poses shock and fire hazards. Replacement plugs are available in different styles to match common appliance cords. Always choose a replacement that is similar to the original plug. Flat-cord and quick-connect plugs are used with light-duty appliances like lamps or radios. Round-cord plugs are used with larger appliances, including those that have three-prong grounding plugs.

Some appliances use polarized plugs. A polarized plug has one wide prong and one narrow prong, corresponding to the hot and neutral slots found in a standard receptacle. Polarization ensures that the cord wires are aligned correctly with the receptacle slots. If there is room in the plug body, tie the individual wires in an underwriter's knot to secure the plug to the cord.

How to Install a Quick-connect Plug

1 Squeeze the prongs of the new quick-connect plug together slightly and pull the plug core from the casing. Cut the old plug from the flat-cord wire with a combination tool, leaving a clean-cut end.

2 Feed unstripped wire through the rear of the plug casing. Spread the prongs, then insert the wire into the rear of the core. Squeeze prongs together; spikes inside the core penetrate the cord. Slide casing over the core until it snaps into place.

How to Replace a Round-cord Plug

1 Cut off round cord near the old plug, using a combination tool. Remove the insulating faceplate on the new plug, and feed the cord through the rear of the plug. Strip about 3" of the outer insulation from the round cord. Strip ¾" insulation from the individual wires.

2 Tie an underwriter's knot with black and white wires (photo below). Make sure knot is located at the edge of the stripped outer insulation. Pull cord so knot slides into plug body.

3 Hook the end of the black wire clockwise around the brass screw, and white wire around the silver screw. On a three-prong plug, attach third wire to grounding screw. If necessary, excess grounding wire can be cut away.

4 Tighten the screws securely, making sure the copper wires do not touch each other. Replace the insulating faceplate.

How to Replace a Flat-cord Plug

1 Cut the old plug from the cord using a combination tool. Pull apart the two halves of the flat cord so that about 2" of wire are separated. Strip ¾" insulation from each half. Remove the casing cover on the new plug.

2 Hook the ends of the wires clockwise around the screws, and tighten them securely (photo below). Reassemble the plug casing. Some plugs may have an insulating faceplate that must be installed.

> **TIP:**
> When replacing a polarized plug, make sure that the ridged half of the cord lines up with the wider (neutral) prong of the plug.

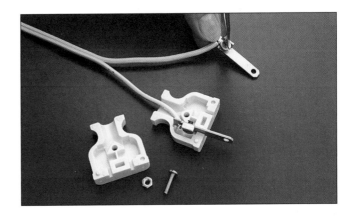

Repairing & Replacing Incandescent Light Fixtures

Incandescent light fixtures are attached permanently to ceilings or walls. They include wall-hung sconces, ceiling-hung globe fixtures, recessed light fixtures and chandeliers. Most incandescent light fixtures are easy to repair, using basic tools and inexpensive parts.

Track lights, another type of incandescent light fixture, are difficult to fix and should be repaired or replaced by an electrician.

RECOMMENDED HAND TOOLS

MASTERCRAFT

BASIC HAND TOOLS

- neon circuit tester
- continuity tester
- combination tool

NEEDED MATERIALS

- replacement parts as needed

If a light fixture fails, always make sure it is screwed in tightly and is not burned out. A faulty light bulb is the most common cause of light fixture failure. If the light fixture is controlled by a wall switch, also check the switch as a possible source of problems.

Light fixtures can fail because the sockets or built-in switches wear out. Some fixtures have sockets and switches that can be removed for minor repairs. The parts are held to the base of the fixture with mounting screws or clips. Other fixtures have sockets and switches that are joined permanently to the base. If this type of fixture fails, purchase and install a new light fixture.

Damage to light fixtures often occurs because homeowners install light bulbs with wattage ratings that are too high. Prevent overheating and light fixture failures by using only light bulbs that match the wattage ratings printed on the fixtures.

In a typical incandescent light fixture, a black hot wire is connected to a brass screw terminal on the socket. Power flows to a small tab on the bottom of the metal socket and through a metal filament inside the bulb. The power heats the filament and causes it to glow. The current then flows through the threaded portion of the socket and through the white neutral wire back to the main service panel.

How to Remove a Light Fixture & Test a Socket

1 Turn off the power to the light fixture at the main service panel. Remove the light bulb and any shade or globe, then remove the mounting screws holding the fixture base to the electrical box or mounting strap. Carefully pull the fixture base away from the box.

2 Test for power by touching one probe of a neon circuit tester to the green grounding screw, then insert the other probe into each wire connector (photo left). The tester should not glow. If it does, there is still power entering the box. Return to the service panel and turn the power off to the correct circuit.

3 Disconnect the light fixture base by loosening the screw terminals (photo opposite page). If the fixture has wire leads instead of screw terminals, remove the light fixture base by unscrewing the wire connectors.

4 Adjust the metal tab at the bottom of the fixture socket by prying it up slightly with a small screwdriver. This adjustment will improve the contact between the socket and the light bulb.

5 Test the socket by attaching the clip of a continuity tester to the hot screw terminal (or black wire lead) and touching the probe of the tester to the metal tab in the bottom of the socket. The tester should glow. If it does not, the socket is faulty and must be replaced.

6 Attach tester clip to neutral terminal (or white wire lead), and touch the probe to the threaded portion of the socket. The tester should glow. If not, the socket is faulty and must be replaced. If the socket is permanently attached, replace the fixture.

How to Test & Replace a Built-in Light Switch

1 Remove the light fixture (steps 1 to 3). Unscrew the retaining ring holding the switch.

2 Label the wires connected to the switch leads. Disconnect the switch leads and remove the switch.

3 Test the switch by attaching the clip of a continuity tester to one of the switch leads and holding tester probe to the other lead. Operate the switch control. If the switch is good, the tester will glow when the switch is in one position, but not in both.

4 If the switch is faulty, purchase and install an exact duplicate. Remount the light fixture, and turn on the power at the main service panel.

How to Replace a Socket

1 Remove the light fixture (steps 1 to 3). Remove the socket from the fixture. The socket may be held by a screw, clip or retaining ring. Disconnect the wires attached to the socket.

2 Purchase an identical replacement. Connect the white wire to the silver screw terminal on the socket, and connect the black wire to the brass screw terminal. Attach the socket to the fixture base, and reinstall the fixture.

TROUBLESHOOTING GUIDE

Problem 1: Wall- or ceiling-mounted fixture flickers or does not light.
Solution: a) Check for faulty light bulb. b) Check wall switch, and repair or replace, if needed. c) Check for loose wire connections in the electrical box. d) Test socket, and replace, if needed. e) Replace the light fixture.

Problem 2: Built-in switch on the fixture does not work.
Solution: a) Check for faulty light bulb. b) Check for loose wire connections in the electrical box. c) Replace the switch. d) Replace the light fixture.

Problem 3: Chandelier flickers or does not light.
Solution: a) Check for a faulty light bulb. b) Check the wall switch, and repair or replace, if needed. c) Check for loose wire connections in the electrical box. d) Test sockets and fixture wires, and replace, if needed.

Problem 4: Recessed fixture flickers or does not light.
Solution: a) Check for faulty light bulb. b) Check wall switch, and repair or replace, if needed. c) Check for loose wire connections in the electrical box. d) Test the fixture, and replace, if needed.

PLUMBING REPAIRS

The plumbing lines running through your home include two separate systems of pipes. The freshwater supply pipes are narrow, ½" to 1" in diameter, feeding water to all parts of your house under pressure. The drain-waste-vent (DWV) lines run through large pipes, 1¼" or more in diameter, into the sewer. The drain system is under no pressure; it operates by the force of gravity.

Nearly all plumbing repairs involve leaks or clogs. Leaks are caused by pressure in the supply system, which puts stress on the pipes, joints and fixtures. Clogs form because of the lack of pressure in the drain.

How to Shut Off the Water & Drain the Pipes

Individual shutoff valves are found on some sinks and most toilets. They are generally located at the supply tubes feeding the fixture. Turn the valve clockwise to stop the water flow, then open the faucet or flush the toilet to release water standing in the lines.

The main shutoff valve, located near the water meter, can be closed to shut off all water. Open faucets at the highest and lowest point in your home to drain the water lines.

TIP:

The First Rule of Successful Plumbing: Shut off the water and drain the pipes before beginning.

90° elbows are used to make right-angle bends in a pipe run. Drain-waste-vent (DWV) elbows are curved to prevent debris from being trapped in the bend.

T-fittings are used to connect branch lines in water supply and drain-waste-vent systems. A T-fitting used in a DWV system is called a "waste-T" or "sanitary-T."

Couplings are used to join two straight pipes. Special transition fittings are used to join two pipes that are made from different material.

Reducers connect pipes of different diameters. Reducing T-fittings and elbows are also available.

45° elbows are used to make gradual bends in a pipe run. Elbows are also available with 60° and 72° bends.

Water supply fittings:
copper (A), galvanized (B), CPVC (C).

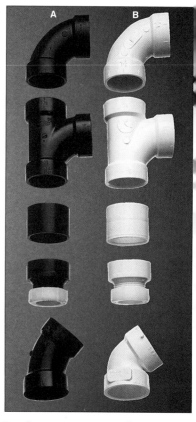

Drain-waste-vent fittings:
ABS (A); PVC (B).

Working with Copper

Copper is the ideal material for water supply pipes. It resists corrosion and has smooth surfaces that provide good water flow. Copper pipes are available in several diameters, but most home water supply systems use ½" or ¾" pipe.

Copper pipe is manufactured in many varieties to be used for different applications. Rigid copper comes in three wall-thickness grades: Types M, L, and K. Type M is the thinnest, Type L is thicker and more rigid and Type K is the thickest. Type K is often used for underground water service lines.

Flexible copper comes in two wall-thickness grades: Types L and K. Both are approved for most home water supply systems, although flexible Type L copper is used primarily for gas service lines. Because it is bendable and will resist a mild frost, Type L may be installed as part of the water supply system in unheated indoor areas, like crawl spaces. Type K is used for underground water service lines.

A third form of copper, called DWV, is used for drain systems. Because most codes now allow low-cost plastic pipes for drain systems, DWV copper is seldom used.

Copper pipes are connected with soldered or compression fittings. Always follow your local Code for the correct type of pipes and fittings allowed in your area.

Grade Stamp Information includes the pipe diameter and the wall-thickness grade. Type M pipe is identified by red lettering, Type L by blue lettering.

How to Cut Rigid & Flexible Copper Pipe

1 Place the tubing cutter over the pipe and tighten the handle so that the pipe rests on both rollers and the cutting wheel is on the marked cutting line.

2 Turn the tubing cutter one rotation so that the cutting wheel scores a continuous straight line around the pipe (photo below).

3 Rotate the cutter in the opposite direction, tightening the handle slightly after every two rotations, until the cut is complete.

4 Remove sharp metal burrs from the inside edge of the cut pipe, using the reaming point on the tubing cutter or a round file.

- coil-spring tubing bender
- wire brush
- flux brush
- tubing cutter
- propane torch
- adjustable wrenches

NEEDED MATERIALS

- pipe joint compound
- self-cleaning soldering paste (flux)
- lead-free solder
- compression fitting
- emery cloth

TIP:

Bend flexible copper pipe using a flexible coil-spring tubing bender to avoid kinks. Select a bender that matches the outside diameter of the pipe. Slip the bender over the pipe using a twisting motion. Bend the pipe slowly until it reaches the desired angle, but not more than 90°.

Safety Tips for Soldering

Use caution when soldering copper pipe. Pipes and fitting become very hot and must be allowed to cool before handling.

Keep the joint dry when soldering existing water pipes by plugging the pipe with bread. Bread absorbs moisture that may ruin the soldering process and cause pinhole leaks. The bread will dissolve when the water is turned back on.

Prevent accidents by shutting off the propane torch immediately after use. Make sure the valve is closed completely.

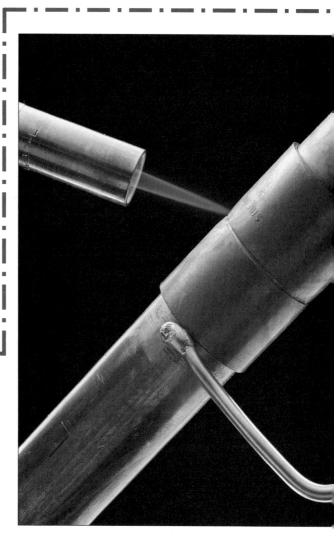

How to Solder Copper Pipes & Fittings

1 Clean the end of each pipe by sanding with a piece of emery cloth. The ends must be free of dirt and grease to ensure that the solder forms a good seal.

2 Clean the inside of each fitting by scouring with a wire brush or emery cloth.

3 Apply a thin layer of soldering paste (flux) to the end of each pipe, using a flux brush. Soldering paste should cover about 1" of the pipe end.

4 Assemble each joint by inserting the pipe fitting so it is tight against the bottom of the fitting sockets. Twist each fitting slightly to spread the soldering paste.

5 Prepare the wire solder by unwinding 8" to 10" of wire from the spool. Bend the first 2" of the wire to a 90° angle.

6 Light the propane torch by opening the valve and striking a spark lighter or match next to the torch nozzle until the gas ignites.

7 Adjust the torch valve until the inner portion of the flame is 1" to 2" long.

8 Hold the flame tip against the middle of the fitting for 4 to 5 seconds, until soldering paste begins to sizzle.

9 Heat the other side of the copper fitting to ensure that the heat is distributed evenly. Touch the solder to the pipe. If the solder melts, the pipe is ready to be soldered (photo above).

10 When the pipe is hot enough to melt the solder, remove the torch and quickly push 1/2" to 3/4" of solder into each joint. Capillary action fills the joint with liquid solder. A correctly soldered joint should show a thin bead of solder around the lip of the fitting.

11 When all the joints have cooled, turn on the water and check for leaks. If the joint leaks, drain the pipes, apply additional soldering paste to the rim of the joint, and resolder.

Using Compression Fittings

Compression fittings are used to make connections that may need to be taken apart. Compression fittings are used most often with flexible copper pipe. Flexible copper is soft enough to let the compression ring seat snugly, creating a watertight seal.

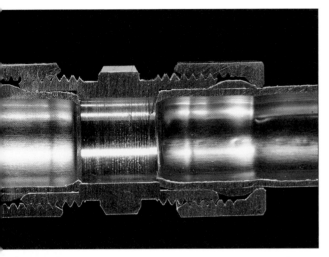

Compression fitting *shows how the threaded compression nut forms a seal by forcing the compression ring against the copper pipe. The compression ring is covered with pipe joint compound before assembling to ensure a perfect seal.*

How to Attach Supply Tubes to Fixture Shutoff Valves with Compression Fittings

1 Bend flexible copper supply tube, and mark the length. Include ½" for the portion of the tube that will fit inside the valve.

2 Slide the compression nut and then the compression ring over the end of the pipe. Threads of the nut should face the valve.

3 Apply a layer of pipe joint compound over the compression ring (photo bottom left). The joint compound helps ensure a watertight seal.

4 Insert the end of the pipe into the fitting, so that it fits flush against the bottom of the fitting socket (photo bottom right).

5 Slide the compression ring and nut against the threads of the valve. Hand-tighten the nut onto the valve.

6 Tighten the compression nut with adjustable wrenches. Do not over-tighten. Turn on the water and watch for leaks. If the fitting leaks, tighten the nut gently.

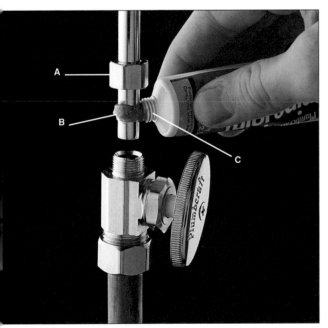

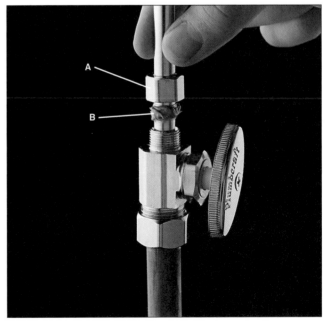

Compression nut (A), *compression ring (B), pipe joint compound (C).*

- felt-tipped pen
- tubing cutter, mitre box, or hacksaw
- groove joint pliers

NEEDED MATERIALS

- plastic pipe
- fittings
- emery cloth
- plastic pipe primer
- solvent glue
- rag
- petroleum jelly

TIP:

Your home electrical system could be grounded through metal water pipes. When adding plastic pipes to a metal plumbing system, make sure the electrical ground circuit is not broken. Use ground clamps and jumper wires, available at any hardware store, to bypass the plastic transition and complete the electrical ground circuit. Clamps must be firmly attached to the bare metal on both sides of the plastic pipe.

Working with Plastic

Plastic pipes and fittings are popular with do-it-yourselfers because they are lightweight, inexpensive and easy to use. Local plumbing Codes increasingly are approving the use of plastics for home plumbing.

Plastic pipes are available in rigid and flexible forms. Rigid plastics include ABS (Acrylonitrile-Butadiene-Styrene), PVC (Poly-Vinyl-Chloride) and CPVC (Chlorinated-Poly-Vinyl-Chloride). The most commonly used flexible plastic is PB (Poly-Butane).

Plastic pipes can be joined to existing iron or copper pipes using transition fittings, but different types of plastic should not be joined. For example, if your drain pipes are ABS plastic, use only ABS pipes and fittings when making repairs.

Prolonged exposure to sunlight eventually can weaken plastic plumbing pipe, so plastics should not be installed or stored in areas that receive constant direct sunlight.

Plastic Pipe Grade Stamps

Material identification: For sink traps and drain pipes, use PVC or ABS pipe. For water supply pipes, use PB or CPVC pipe.

For sink traps and drains, choose PVC or ABS pipe that has DWV (drain-waste-vent) rating by the CSA (Canadian Standards Association). For water supply pipes, choose PB or CPVC pipe that has PW (pressurized water) rating.

Pipe diameter: PVC and ABS pipes for drains usually have an inside diameter of 1¼" to 4". PB and CPVC pipes for water supply usually have an inside diameter of ½" or ¾".

Solvent-glued fittings are used on rigid plastic pipes. The solvent dissolves a thin layer of plastic and bonds the pipe and fitting together.

Grip fittings are used to join flexible PB pipes and can also be used for CPVC pipes. Grip fittings come in two styles. One type resembles a copper compression fitting. It has a metal grip ring and a plastic compression ring. The other type has a rubber O-ring instead of a compression ring.

Cutting & Fitting Plastic Pipe

Tighten a tubing cutter around the pipe so that the cutting wheel is on the marked line. Rotate the tool around the pipe, tightening the screw every two rotations, until the pipe snaps. A hacksaw or mitre box can also be used to cut plastic pipe.

How to Solvent-glue Rigid Plastic Pipe

1 Remove any rough burrs on the cut ends of the plastic pipe, using a utility knife.

2 Test-fit all pipes and fittings. The pipes should fit tightly against the bottom of the fitting sockets.

3 Make alignment marks across each joint with a felt-tipped pen.

4 Mark the depth of the fitting sockets on pipes. Take the pipes apart.

5 Clean the ends of the pipes and the fitting sockets with an emery cloth.

6 Apply the plastic pipe primer to the ends of the pipes. The primer dulls the glossy surfaces and ensures a good seal.

7 Apply the plastic pipe primer to the insides of the fitting sockets.

8 Solvent-glue each joint by applying a thick coat of solvent glue to the end of the pipe. Apply a thin coat of solvent glue to the inside surface of the fitting socket. **WORK QUICKLY:** Solvent glue hardens in about 30 seconds.

9 Quickly position the pipe and fitting so that the alignment marks are offset about 2" (photo right). Force the pipe into the fitting until the end fits flush against the bottom of the socket. Twist the pipe into alignment.

10 Spread the solvent by twisting the pipe until the marks are aligned. Hold the pipe in place for about 20 seconds to prevent the joint from slipping.

11 Wipe away excess solvent with a rag. Do not disturb the joint for 30 minutes.

TIP:
Find the length of pipe needed by measuring between the bottoms of the fitting sockets. Mark the length on the pipe with a felt-tipped pen.

How to Cut & Fit Flexible Plastic Pipe

1 Cut the flexible PB pipe with a plastic tubing cutter. (Flexible pipe can also be cut with a mitre box or sharp knife.) Remove any rough burrs with a utility knife.

2 Take each grip fitting apart and make sure that the grip ring and the compression ring or O-ring are positioned properly. Loosely reassemble the fitting.

3 Make a mark on the pipe showing the depth of the fitting socket, using a felt-tipped pen. Round off the edges of the pipe with emery cloth.

4 Lubricate the end of the pipe with petroleum jelly. A lubricated tip makes it easier to insert the pipes into the grip fittings.

5 Force the end of the pipe into the fitting up to the mark on the pipe. Hand-tighten the coupling nut.

6 Tighten the coupling nut about ½ turn with groove joint pliers. Turn on the water and test the fitting. If the fitting leaks, tighten the coupling nut slightly.

Parts of a grip fitting: *coupling nut (A), grip ring (B), compression ring (C).*

Faucet Problems & Repairs

Faucet problems are common, but fortunately they are easy to fix. Replacement parts for faucet repairs are usually quite inexpensive and are readily available.

If a badly worn faucet continues to leak even after you make attempts to repair it, replacing it with a new model is the best option. The ingenious designs used in modern faucets allow these fixtures to provide years of trouble-free service. A good-quality faucet set may last longer than any other element in your bathroom or kitchen.

TROUBLESHOOTING GUIDE

Problem 1: Faucet drips from the end of the spout or leaks around the base.
Solution: Identify the faucet design, then purchase and install replacement parts.

Problem 2: Old, worn-out faucet repeatedly develops leaks after it is fixed.
Solution: Replace the old faucet with a reliable modern design.

Problem 3: Water pressure at the spout seems low or the water flow is partially blocked.
Solution: a) Clean the faucet aerator.
b) Replace the old galvanized steel pipes with copper pipes.

Problem 4: Water leaks onto the floor beneath the faucet.
Solution: a) Inspect the sprayer hose and replace it if cracked. b) Tighten all the water connections, or replace the supply tubes and shutoff valves. c) Inspect the sink strainer, and replace it, if necessary.

Identifying Your Faucet Type

Ball-type faucet

Cartridge faucet

Ceramic disc faucet

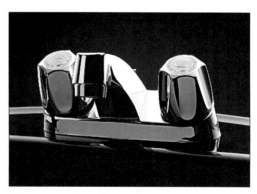

Compression faucet

Fixing Ball-type Faucets

A ball-type faucet has a single handle and is identified by the hollow metal or plastic ball inside the faucet body. Many ball-type faucets have a rounded cap with knurled edges located under the handle. If your faucet leaks from the spout and has this type of cap, first try tightening the cap with groove joint pliers. If tightening does not fix the leak, disas-semble the faucet and install replacement parts.

Replace the rotating ball only if it is obviously worn or scratched. Replacement balls are either metal or plastic. Metal balls are slightly more expensive than plastic, but more durable. **Remember to turn off the water before beginning work.**

RECOMMENDED HAND TOOLS

MASTERCRAFT

BASIC HAND TOOLS

- groove joint pliers
- allen wrench

How to Fix a Ball-type Faucet

1 Loosen the handle screw-set with an allen wrench. Remove the handle to expose the faucet cap.

2 Remove the cap with groove joint pliers. To prevent scratches to the shiny chromed finish, wrap masking tape around the jaws of the pliers.

3 Lift out the faucet cam, cam washer and the rotating ball. Check the ball for signs of wear.

4 Reach into the faucet with a screwdriver and remove the old springs and neoprene valve seats (photo top right).

5 Remove the spout by twist-ing it upward, then cut off the old O-rings. Coat the new O-rings with heatproof grease, and install. Reattach the spout, pressing downward until the collar rests on the plastic slip ring. Install the new springs and valve seats.

6 Insert the ball, new cam washer and cam. The small lug on the cam should fit into the notch on the faucet body (photo bottom right). Screw the cap onto the faucet and reattach the handle.

Valve seat (A), springs (B).

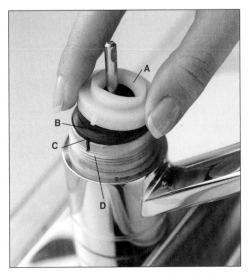

Cam (A), lug (B), cam washer (C), notch (D).

NEEDED MATERIALS

- ball-type faucet repair kit
- new rotating ball (if needed)
- masking tape
- O-rings
- heatproof grease

TIP:

Most faucet repairs require only Master-craft groove joint pliers, utility knife and screwdriver set.

MASTERCRAFT

BASIC HAND TOOLS

- groove joint pliers

NEEDED MATERIALS

- replacement cartridge
- O-rings
- heatproof grease

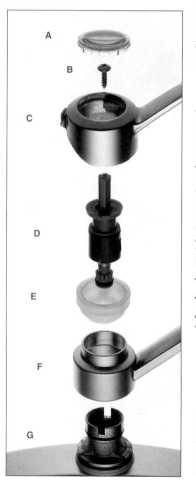

A

B

C

D

E

F

G

Cartridge faucet: *index cap (A), handle screw (B), handle (C), cartridge (D), retaining ring (E), spout (F), O-rings (G).*

Fixing Cartridge Faucets

The cartridge faucet can be identified by the narrow metal or plastic cartridge inside the faucet body that lifts and rotates to control the flow and temperature of the water. The cartridge faucet is available in single- and double-handled models. In single-handled cartridge faucets, one large cartridge is used; in double-handled cartridge faucets, two smaller cartridges are used.

As with other faucet styles, leaks in the cartridge faucet can most commonly be attributed to worn, dirty or cracked O-rings and seals. When opening the faucet to check the seals, O-rings or to replace the cartridge, it is a good idea to replace the O-rings that seal the joint between the body of the faucet and the rotating spout.

When replacing the cartridge, make sure that you insert the new cartridge so that it is aligned in the same way the previous cartridge was aligned. You will find that your hot and cold water controls are reversed if inserted incorrectly. Should you find this happening, open the faucet and turn the cartridge 180°. **Remember to turn the water off before you begin your repairs.**

How to Fix a Cartridge Faucet

1 Pry off the index cap on top of the faucet, and remove the handle screw underneath the cap.

2 Remove the faucet handle by lifting it up and tilting it backwards.

3 Remove the threaded retaining ring with groove joint pliers. Remove any retaining clip holding the cartridge into place.

4 Grip the top of the cartridge with groove joint pliers. Pull straight up to remove the cartridge. Install the replacement cartridge so that the tab on the cartridge faces forward.

5 Remove the spout by pulling up and twisting, then cut off the old O-rings with a utility knife. Coat the new O-rings with heatproof grease, and install.

6 Reattach the spout. Screw the retaining ring onto the faucet, and tighten with groove joint pliers. Attach the handle, handle screw and index cap.

Fixing Ceramic Disc Faucets

A ceramic disc faucet has a single handle and is identified by a wide cylinder inside the faucet body. The cylinder contains a pair of closely fitting ceramic discs that control the flow of water.

A ceramic disc faucet is a top-quality fixture that is easy to repair. Leaks usually can be fixed by lifting out the cylinder and cleaning the neoprene seals and cylinder openings. Install a new cylinder only if the faucet continues to leak after cleaning.

After making repairs to a disc faucet, make sure the handle is in the ON position, then open the shutoff valves slowly. Otherwise, ceramic discs can be cracked by the sudden release of air from the faucet. When the water runs steadily, close the faucet. **Remember to turn off the water before beginning work.**

How to Fix a Ceramic Disc Faucet

1 Rotate the faucet spout to the side, and raise the handle. Remove the set screw and lift off the handle.

2 Remove the escutcheon cap. Remove the cartridge mounting screws, and lift out the cylinder.

3 Remove the neoprene seals from the cylinder openings.

4 Clean the cylinder openings and the neoprene seals with an abrasive pad. Rinse the cylinder with clear water.

5 Return the seals to the cylinder opening, and reassemble the faucet. Move the handle to the ON position, then slowly open the shutoff valves. When the water runs steadily, close the faucet.

RECOMMENDED HAND TOOLS

MASTERCRAFT

BASIC HAND TOOLS

NEEDED MATERIALS

• replacement cylinder (if needed)
• abrasive pad

TIP:
Take old faucet parts with you to the store to be sure you obtain proper replacements.

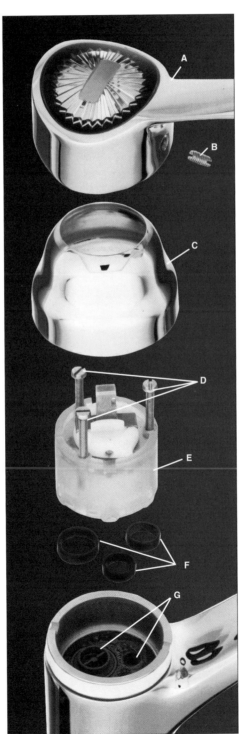

Ceramic disc faucet: handle (A), set screw (B), escutcheon cap (C), mounting screws (D), ceramic disc cylinder (E), neoprene seals (F), water inlets (G).

RECOMMENDED HAND TOOLS

MASTERCRAFT

BASIC HAND TOOLS

- handle puller
- groove joint pliers

NEEDED MATERIALS

- universal washer kit
- packing string
- heatproof grease
- replacement valve seats

TIP:

Remove stubborn handles with a handle puller. Remove the faucet index cap and handle screw, and clamp the side bars of the puller under the handle. Thread the puller into the faucet stem, and tighten until the handle comes free.

Fixing Compression Faucets

Compression faucets have separate controls for hot and cold water and are identified by the threaded stem assemblies inside the faucet body.

Older compression faucets often have corroded handles that are difficult to remove. A specialty tool called a handle puller makes this job easier. Handle pullers may be available at rental centres.

Compression stems come in many different styles, but all have some type of neoprene washer or seal to control the water flow. Compression faucets leak when the stem washers and seals become worn.

When replacing washers, also check the condition of the metal valve seats inside the faucet body. If the valve seats feel rough, they should be replaced or resurfaced. **Remember to turn off the water before beginning work.**

A universal washer kit contains parts needed to fix most types of compression faucets. Choose a kit that has an assortment of neoprene washers, O-rings, packing washers and brass stem screws.

How to Fix a Compression Faucet

1 Remove the index cap from the top of the faucet handle, and remove the handle screw. Remove the handle by pulling straight up. If necessary, use a handle puller to remove the handle.

2 Unscrew the stem assembly from the body of the faucet, using groove joint pliers. Inspect the valve seat for wear, and replace or resurface as needed. If the faucet body or stems are badly worn, it is usually best to replace the faucet.

3 Remove the brass stem screw from the stem assembly (photo bottom left). Remove the worn stem washer.

4 Unscrew the threaded spindle from the retaining nut (photo bottom right).

5 Cut off O-ring and replace with an exact duplicate. Install a new washer and stem screw. Coat all the parts with heatproof grease, then reassemble the faucet.

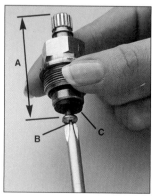

Stem assembly (A), *brass stem screw (B), stem washer (C).*

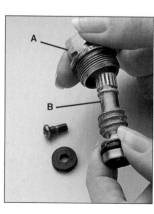

Retaining nut (A), *threaded spindle (B).*

Common Toilet Problems

A clogged toilet is one of the most common plumbing problems. If the toilet overflows or flushes sluggishly, clear the clog with a plunger or closet auger. If the problem persists, the clog may be in the main waste and vent stack.

A recurring puddle of water on the floor around the toilet may be caused by a crack in the toilet base or in the tank. A damaged toilet should be replaced. Installing a new toilet is an easy project that can be finished in three or four hours.

A standard two-piece toilet has an upper tank that is bolted to the base. This type of toilet uses a simple gravity-operated flush system. Some one-piece toilets use a complicated, high-pressure flush valve. Repairing these toilets can be difficult, so this work should be left to a professional.

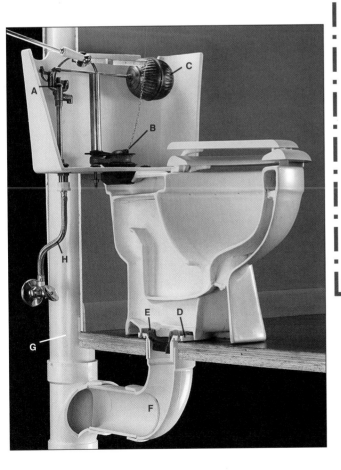

Typical Toilet: *ballcock (A), flush valve (B), float ball (C), toilet flange (D), wax ring (E), closet bend (F), main waste and vent stack (G), cold water supply tube (H).*

TROUBLESHOOTING GUIDE

Problem 1: Toilet handle sticks or is hard to push.
Solution: a) Adjust the lift wires. b) Clean and adjust the handle.

Problem 2: Handle is loose.
Solution: a) Adjust the handle. b) Reattach the lift chain or lift wires to the lever.

Problem 3: Toilet will not flush at all.
Solution: a) Make sure the water is turned on. b) Adjust the lift chains or lift wires.

Problem 4: Toilet does not flush completely.
Solution: a) Adjust the lift chain.
b) Adjust the water level in the tank.

Problem 5: Toilet overflows, or flushes sluggishly.
Solution: a) Clear the clogged toilet.
b) Clear clogged main waste and vent stack.

Problem 6: Toilet runs continuously.
Solution: a) Adjust the lift wires or lift chain. b) Replace leaky float ball. c) Adjust the water level in the tank. d) Adjust and clean the flush valve. e) Replace the flush valve. f) Repair or replace the ballcock.

Problem 7: Water on the floor around the toilet.
Solution: a) Tighten the tank bolts and water connections. b) Insulate the tank to prevent condensation. c) Replace the wax ring. d) Replace cracked tank or bowl.

RECOMMENDED HAND TOOLS

- adjustable wrench
- needlenose pliers
- small wire brush

NEEDED MATERIALS

- vinegar

Minor Adjustments

Minor adjustments made to the handle or the attached chain (or wires) will solve many minor toilet problems. Sticky handles, continuously running toilets and toilets that will not flush properly can all be attributed to minor handle and lift chain problems. Start repairs by adjusting and cleaning the handle and lift chain mechanisms.

Adjusting a Toilet Handle & Lift Chain (or Lift Wires)

Clean and adjust the handle mounting nut so the handle operates smoothly. The mounting nut has reversed threads. Loosen the nut by turning it clockwise; tighten by turning counterclockwise. Remove any lime build-up by scrubbing the handle parts with a brush dipped in vinegar.

Adjust the lift chain so that it hangs straight from the handle lever, with about ½" of slack. Remove excess slack in the chain by hooking the chain in a different hole in the handle lever, or by removing links with needlenose pliers. A broken lift chain must be replaced.

Adjust lift wires (found on toilets without lift chains) so that the wires are straight and operate smoothly when the handle is pushed. A sticky handle often can be fixed by straightening bent lift wires.

RECOMMENDED HAND TOOLS

- small wire brush
- adjustable wrenches
- spud wrench or groove joint pliers

NEEDED MATERIALS

- universal washer kit
- ballcock
- ballcock seals
- emery cloth
- sponge
- abrasive pad
- flapper or tank ball
- flush valve

Fixing a Running Toilet

The sound of continuously running water can be caused by several different problems: if the lift wire (or lift chain) is bent or nicked; if the float ball leaks or rubs against the side of the tank; if a faulty ballcock does not shut off the fresh water supply; or if the flush valve allows water to leak down the toilet bowl. First, check the lift wires and float ball. If making simple adjustments and repairs to these parts does not fix the problem, then you will need to repair the ballcock or flush valve.

Check the overflow pipe if the sound of running water continues after the float ball and lift wires are adjusted. If you see water flowing into the overflow pipe, the ballcock needs to be repaired. First, adjust ballcock to lower the water level in the tank. If the problem continues, repair or replace the ballcock. If the water is not flowing into the overflow pipe, then the flush valve needs to be repaired. First check the tank ball (or flapper) for wear, and replace if necessary. If the problem continues, replace the flush valve.

Adjusting a Ballcock to Set Water Level

A traditional plunger-valve ballcock is made of brass. The water flow is controlled by a plunger attached to the float arm and ball. Lower the water level by bending the float arm down slightly. Raise the water level by bending the float arm up slightly.

A diaphragm ballcock is usually made of plastic and has a wide bonnet that contains a rubber diaphragm. Lower the water level by bending the float arm down slightly. Raise the water level by bending the float arm upward.

A float cup ballcock is made of plastic and is easy to adjust. Lower the water level by pinching the spring clip on the pull rod and moving the float cup downward on the ballcock shank. Raise the water level by moving the cup upward.

A floatless ballcock controls the water level with a pressure-sensing device. Lower the water level by turning the adjustment screw counterclockwise, a half turn at a time. Raise the water level by turning the screw clockwise. Floatless ballcocks are repair-free, but eventually they may need to be replaced.

How to Repair a Diaphragm Ballcock

1 Shut off the water, and flush the toilet to empty the tank. Remove the screws from the bonnet.

2 Lift the float arm with bonnet attached. Check the diaphragm and plunger for wear.

3 Replace any stiff or cracked parts. If the assembly is badly worn, replace the entire ballcock.

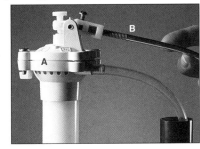

Diaphragm ballcock:
bonnet (A), float arm (B).

How to Repair a Float Cup Ballcock

1 Shut off the water, and flush to empty the tank. Remove the ballcock cap.

2 Remove the bonnet by pushing and turning counterclockwise. Clean out sediment inside the ballcock with a wire brush.

3 Replace the seal. If the assembly is badly worn, replace the entire ballcock.

Float cup ballcock:
float cup (A),
shank (B),
pull rod (C),
spring clip (D).

How to Repair a Plunger-valve Ballcock

1 Shut off the water, and flush to empty the tank. Remove the wing nuts on the ballcock. Slip out the float arm.

2 Pull up on the plunger to remove it. Pry out the packing washer or O-ring. Pry out the plunger washer. (Remove the stem screw, if necessary.)

3 Install replacement washers. Clean sediment from inside the ballcock with a wire brush. Reassemble the ballcock.

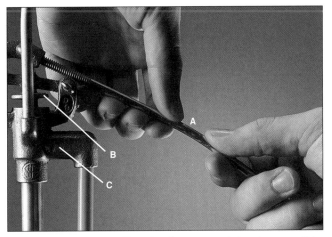

Plunger-valve ballcock: *float arm (A), plunger (B), ballcock (C).*

How to Install a New Ballcock

1 Shut off the water, and flush the toilet to empty the tank. Use a sponge to remove the remaining water. Disconnect supply tube coupling nut with an adjustable wrench. Remove old ballcock.

2 Attach cone washer to new ballcock tailpiece. Insert tailpiece into tank opening.

3 Align the float arm socket so float arm will pass behind the overflow pipe. Screw float arm onto ballcock and float ball onto the float arm.

4 Bend or clip the refill tube so the tip is inside the overflow pipe.

5 Screw the mounting nut and coupling nut onto the ballcock tailpiece, and tighten with an adjustable wrench. Turn on the water, and check for leaks.

6 Adjust water level in tank so it is about 1/2" below the top of the overflow pipe.

How to Install a New Flush Valve

1 Shut off water, disconnect ballcock, and remove toilet tank. Remove old flush valve by unscrewing spud nut with a spud wrench or groove joint pliers.

2 Slide cone washer onto tailpiece of new flush valve. The bevelled side of the cone washer should face the end of the tailpiece. Insert the flush valve into the tank opening so that the overflow pipe faces the ballcock.

3 Screw spud nut onto tailpiece of flush valve, and tighten with a spud wrench or groove joint pliers. Place soft spud washer over tailpiece, and reinstall toilet tank.

RECOMMENDED HAND TOOLS

- adjustable wrench
- putty knife
- ratchet wrench
- groove joint pliers

NEEDED MATERIALS

- rag
- tank liner kit
- abrasive cleaner
- wax ring
- plumber's putty
- sponge
  For new installation:
- new toilet
- toilet handle
- ballcock
- flush valve
- tank bolts
- soft spud washer

Fixing a Leaky Toilet

Water leaking onto the floor around a toilet must be fixed to avoid damaging the subfloor. Make sure all the connections are tight. If moisture drips from the tank during humid weather, it is probably condensation. Fix "sweating" by insulating the inside of the tank with foam panels (toilet liner kit). Shut off the water, drain tank, and clean the inside of the tank with an abrasive cleanser. Cut plastic foam panels to fit the bottom, sides, front and back of the tank. Attach panels to the tank with adhesive (included in kit). Cure adhesive as directed.

Water seeping around the base of the toilet can be caused by an old wax ring that no longer seals the drain, or by a cracked toilet base. If leaking occurs during or just after a flush, replace the wax ring. If leaking is constant, the toilet base is cracked and must be replaced. Tighten all connections slightly. Tighten nuts on the tank bolts with a ratchet wrench. Tighten ballcock mounting nut and supply tube coupling nut with an adjustable wrench. Do not overtighten tank bolts, as you may crack the toilet tank.

Adjusting & Cleaning a Flush Valve

Adjust the tank ball (or flapper) so it is directly over the flush valve. The tank ball has a guide arm that can be loosened so the tank ball can be positioned. (Some tank balls have a ball guide that helps seat the tank ball into the flush valve.) Replace the tank ball if it is cracked or worn. Tank balls have a threaded fitting that screws onto lift wire. Clean the opening of the flush valve, using an emery cloth (for brass valves) or an abrasive pad (for plastic valves). Replace flapper if it is worn. Flappers are attached to small lugs on the sides of overflow pipe.

How to Remove & Replace a Wax Ring & Toilet

1 Turn off water, and flush to empty the toilet tank. Use a sponge to remove the remaining water in tank and bowl. Disconnect supply tube with an adjustable wrench.

2 Remove the nuts from the tank bolts with a ratchet wrench. Carefully remove the tank and set it aside.

3 Pry off the floor bolt trim caps at the base of the toilet. Remove the floor nuts with an adjustable wrench.

4 Straddle the toilet and rock the bowl from side to side until the seal breaks. Carefully lift the toilet off the floor bolts and set it on its side. A small amount of water may spill from the toilet trap.

5 Remove the old wax from the toilet flange in the floor. Plug the drain opening with a damp rag to prevent sewer gases from rising into the house.

6 If the old toilet will be reused, clean the old wax and putty from the outlet and base of the toilet.

7 Turn the stool upside down. Place a new wax ring over the drain outlet. If the ring has a rubber or plastic sleeve, the sleeve should face away from the toilet. Apply a bead of plumber's putty to the bottom edge of the toilet base.

8 Position the toilet over the drain so that the floor bolts fit through the openings in the base of the toilet. Thread washers and nuts onto the floor bolts, and tighten with adjustable wrench until snug.

9 Press down on the toilet base to compress wax and putty. Retighten the floor nuts until snug. **CAUTION:** Overtightening the nuts may crack the base.

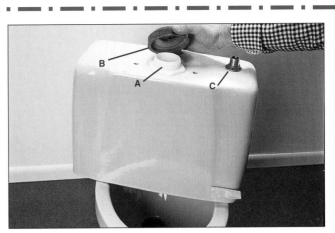

Flush valve tailpiece (A), spud washer (B), ballcock tailpiece (C).

Wipe away excess plumber's putty. Cover nuts with trim caps.

10 Prepare the tank for installation. If necessary, install a handle, ballcock and flush valve. Carefully turn the tank upside down and place a soft spud washer over the flush valve tailpiece (photo above).

11 Turn the tank right side up and position it on the rear of the toilet base so that the spud washer is centred in the water inlet opening.

12 Line up tank bolt holes with holes in the base of the toilet. Slide rubber washers onto tank bolts and place the bolts through the holes. From underneath the tank, thread washers and nuts onto bolts.

13 Tighten the nuts with a ratchet wrench until the tank is snug (photo left). Use caution when tightening the nuts: most toilet tanks rest on the spud washer, not directly on the toilet base.

14 Attach the water supply tube to the ballcock tailpiece with an adjustable wrench. Turn on the water and test the toilet. Tighten the tank bolts and water connections if necessary.

15 Position new toilet seat, if needed, inserting seat bolts into the mounting holes in the toilet. Screw the mounting nuts onto the seat bolts, and tighten.

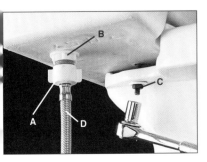

Coupling nut (A), ballcock mounting nut (B), tank bolt (C), supply tube (D).

MASTERCRAFT

BASIC HAND TOOLS

- plunger or hand auger
- small wire brush
- groove joint pliers
- spud wrench
- putty knife

NEEDED MATERIALS

- replacement gaskets
- plumber's putty
- bucket
- rag

Clearing Clogs & Fixing Drains

Clear a clogged drain with a plunger or hand auger. A plunger breaks up clogs by forcing air pressure into the drain line. Because a plunger is effective and easy to use, it should be the first choice for clearing a clog.

A hand auger has a flexible steel cable that is pushed into the drain line to break up or remove obstructions. An auger is easy to use, but for the best results the user must know the "feel" of the cable in the drain line. A little experience is often necessary to tell the difference between a soap clog and a bend in the drain line. Use caustic, acid-based chemical drain cleaners only as a last resort. These drain cleaners, usually available at hardware stores and supermarkets, will dissolve clogs, but they may also damage pipes and must be handled with caution. Always read the manufacturer's directions completely.

Clearing Clogged Sinks

Every sink has a drain trap and fixture drain line. Sink clogs usually are caused by a build-up of soap and hair in the trap or fixture drain line. Remove the clogs by using a plunger, disconnecting and cleaning the trap, or using a hand auger.

Many sinks hold water with a mechanical plug called a pop-up stopper. If the sink will not hold standing water or if the water in the sink drains too slowly, the pop-up stopper must be cleaned and adjusted.

How to Clear Sink Drains with a Plunger

1 Remove drain stopper. Some pop-up stoppers lift out directly; others turn counterclockwise. On some older types, the pivot rod must be removed to free the stopper.

2 Stuff a wet rag in sink overflow opening. The rag prevents air from breaking the suction of the plunger. Place plunger cup over drain and run enough water to cover the rubber cup. Move the plunger handle up and down rapidly to break up the clog.

How to Remove & Clean a Sink Drain Trap

1 Place a bucket under the trap to catch water and debris. Loosen the slip nuts on the trap bend with groove joint pliers. Unscrew nuts by hand and pull off trap bend.

2 Dump out debris. Clean trap bend with a small wire brush. Inspect slip nut washers for wear, and replace if necessary. Reinstall the trap bend, and tighten the slip nuts.

How to Fix Leaky Sink Strainers

1 Unscrew slip nuts from both ends of tailpiece, using groove joint pliers. Disconnect and remove tailpiece from strainer body and trap bend.

2 Remove the locknut, using a spud wrench. Unscrew locknut completely and remove strainer assembly.

3 Remove old putty from drain opening, using a putty knife. If reusing old strainer body, clean off old putty from under the flange. Replace old gaskets and washers.

4 Apply a bead of plumber's putty to lip of drain opening. Press strainer body into drain opening. From under the sink, place the rubber gasket, then metal or fibre friction ring, over the strainer. Reinstall the locknut and tighten. Reinstall the tailpiece.

How to Clear a Fixture Drain Line with a Hand Auger

1 Remove trap. Push end of auger cable into drain line opening until resistance is met. Resistance usually indicates the end of the cable has reached a bend in the pipe.

2 Set auger lock so at least 6" of cable extends out the opening. Crank auger handle clockwise to move the end of the cable past the bend in the drain line.

3 Release lock and continue pushing cable into opening until firm resistance is felt. Set auger lock and crank the handle clockwise. Solid resistance that prevents the cable from advancing indicates a clog. Some clogs, such as a sponge or an accumulation of hair, can be snagged and retrieved (step 4). Continuous resistance that allows cable to advance slowly could be a soap clog (step 5).

4 Pull obstruction out by releasing auger lock and cranking handle clockwise. If no object can be retrieved, reconnect trap bend and use auger to clear nearest branch drain line or main waste and vent stack.

5 Continuous resistance indicates a soap clog. Bore through clog by cranking the auger handle clockwise and applying steady pressure on hand grip of auger. Repeat two or three times. Retrieve cable. Reconnect trap bend and flush system with hot tap water to remove the debris.

TIP:
Regular maintenance helps keep drains working properly. Flush drains once each week with hot tap water to keep them free of soap, grease and debris. Or treat drains once every six months with a non-caustic (copper sulfide or sodium hydroxide-based) drain cleaner. A non-caustic cleaner will not harm the pipes.

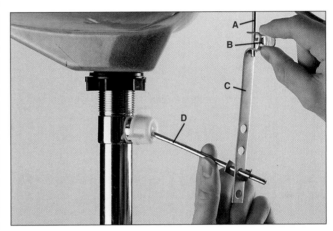

Stopper rod (A), *clevis screw (B), clevis (C), pivot rod (D).*

How to Clean & Adjust a Pop-up Sink Drain Stopper

1 Raise stopper level to full upright (closed) position. Unscrew retaining nut that holds the pivot rod in position. Pull pivot rod out of drain pipe to release stopper.

2 Remove the stopper. Clean debris from the stopper, using a small wire brush. Inspect gasket for wear and damage, and replace if necessary. Reinstall the stopper.

3 If sink does not drain properly, adjust the clevis. Loosen clevis screw. Slide the clevis up or down on the stopper rod to adjust the position of the stopper. Tighten the clevis screw (photo above).

The Mastercraft tools and accessories featured in this book have been provided by Canadian Tire. Visit a Canadian Tire Store near you for a wide assortment of Mastercraft tools and accessories to assist you in your home repair, maintenance and improvement projects.

Index